"In his new book, Dr. Ned Hallowell administers his trademark dose of empathetic wisdom and practical advice about how to live a working life that's sane, successful, and fulfilling in today's hyper-caffeinated, always-on world. By treating attention as our scarcest resource, Hallowell teaches us, through compelling storytelling and thoughtful prescription, how to focus our minds to achieve more, work less, and experience every moment to its fullest. *Driven to Distraction at Work* is an essential survival guide to life in the modern world. Don't wait. You need to read this book now."

—JEFFREY F. RAYPORT, faculty, Harvard Business School; strategic advisor; and investor

"As business continues to be about quality, speed, and focus, competitive advantage will come to those who analyze their abilities and find the best tools available to be most productive. Dr. Hallowell's stunning new book takes the maze of distraction at work away forever!"

—LARRY WEBER, Chairman and CEO, Racepoint Global; founder, Weber Shandwick; and bestselling author, *Marketing to the Social Web*

"If you feel like you never have time to do the things you want or, for that matter, to even *think* about the things you might want—get this book. Dr. Hallowell provides insightful, concrete ideas and suggestions based on the latest research to better manage your life, your business, and your relationships by learning how to make your environment work for you, rather than against you. Applying even a few simple prescriptions most relevant to your needs will dramatically enhance your life and the lives of all with whom you interact."

—DAN L. MONROE, Rose-Marie and Eijk van Otterloo Executive Director and CEO, Peabody Essex Museum

"From America's most praised scholar on the subject, *Driven to Distraction at Work* is overdue and urgently needed common sense on how to master digital detox and eliminate other distractions at work. A must-read for any and all of us who cherish our ability to connect deeply with others as well as to think."

> —MARIE BRENNER, author, *Apples and Oranges*; writer-at-large, *Vanity Fair*

"Who among us doesn't find themselves overwhelmed by details, lacking in consistent focus, oddly connectedly disconnected, and perplexed as to why we are not more robustly productive? This book provides explanations, antidotes, and solutions so important that it should be required reading for everyone. Dr. Hallowell easily translates complex issues into graspable terms. Read this book—it will change your life!"

> —ELLEN MILEY PERRY, author, *A Wealth of Possibilities*; founder, Wealthbridge Partners

"Through compelling stories and a provocative theoretical framework, Dr. Hallowell draws upon decades of experience as a 'focus doctor' to create practical solutions for the ubiquitous problem of distraction and overload in the modern workplace. Read this book and regain the focus you've inadvertently given away."

> —SUZY WELCH, *New York Times* bestselling author, *10-10-10: A Life-Transforming Idea*

"Dr. Hallowell's prescriptions for managing the world of distractions we all face will become the stepping stones for how future generations harness technology while maintaining the deepest human advantage—the ability to think and progress. Readers of *Driven to Distraction at Work* will gain a significant advantage in their ability to manage an always-on environment with a need to creatively think and problem solve. Productivity is the long-term strategic advantage in today's world, and Dr. Hallowell clearly defines the road map to that advantage—getting things done."

—TIM ARMSTRONG, Chairman and CEO, AOL

"Do you think it's possible to truly be focused and productive at your work? In this groundbreaking book, Ned Hallowell tells you how to overcome the inner obstacles that derail your efforts to be your best."

—JOHN BOWEN, founder and CEO, CEG Worldwide, LLC

"Dr. Hallowell has been our leading 'focus doctor' for decades. In this groundbreaking work, he tackles one of the most pressing problems of our era: distraction at work. With vivid, compelling stories, Hallowell provides exceptionally intelligent and extremely actionable solutions to this major modern dilemma. A game-changing read for your life and your business."

—STEVEN KOTLER, author, *The Rise of Superman: Decoding the Science of Ultimate Human Performance*

"Do you feel overwhelmed, rushed, or distractible? Are you finding yourself more and more impatient, dissatisfied, frustrated, and frenzied? Then read *Driven to Distraction at Work*. Dr. Hallowell provides a proven plan for focusing at work and being more productive. This book has techniques, tips, and takeaways you can use to consistently rise above the chaos, find focus, and achieve your goals. If you want to take back control of your attention—and be happier and healthier—this book shows you how."

—JOE POLISH, founder, Genius Network

"The world's foremost expert on attention and focus issues tells us everything we need to know about 'attention deficit trait': a focus-robbing, output-draining syndrome that information and technology overload are inflicting on workers and companies across the business world today. All executives concerned about their employees' well-being and their enterprises' productivity should tear themselves away from their screens long enough to read this book."

—LINDA GOSDEN ROBINSON, global marketing and communications expert

"Ned Hallowell's books are all game changers—and this one tops the others. Hallowell provides a totally contrarian perspective and liberating approach to defeating distraction at work. The secret to success lies in creating daily structures and processes that enable highly distractible individuals to focus on the biggest and best possible results in every situation."

—DAN SULLIVAN, founder and President, The Strategic Coach Inc.

"Millions of readers rely on Dr. Hallowell, the 'focus doctor,' for guidance on this important topic. Hallowell says, 'If you don't take your time, it will be taken from you.' With humor and anecdotes we can all relate to, Hallowell offers a fun read and a practical path for tapping into one's best at work."

—LINDA STONE, former Vice President, Microsoft

driven to distraction at work

driven to distraction at work

HOW TO FOCUS AND BE MORE PRODUCTIVE

Edward M. Hallowell, MD

HARVARD BUSINESS REVIEW PRESS

Boston, Massachusetts

Library of Congress Cataloging-in-Publication Data

Hallowell, Edward M.
  Driven to distraction at work : how to focus and be more productive / Ned Hallowell.
    pages cm
  ISBN 978-1-4221-8641-1 (hardback)
  1. Distraction (Psychology) 2. Attention. 3. Time management. 4. Psychology, Industrial. I. Title.
  BF323.D5H35 2015
  158.7--dc23

                                                                    2014030018

ISBN: 9781422186411

eISBN: 9781422186428

For Tom Bliss: surgeon, fisherman,
father, and friend

CONTENTS

PART TWO

training your attention

how to manage and maintain your ability to focus

attention deficit trait

the growing workplace problem

You know the problem—swarms of distractions, constant interruptions, various tones chiming all around, rampant "screen sucking," texting under the table during meetings, the overloading of mental circuits, and frequent feelings of frustration at trying to get everything done well and on time. This is the modern context in which most of us work. Whether the workplace itself or the numerous demands on your time drive you to distraction, the end result is the same. You can't focus on anything anymore at work, and it's taking its toll on your performance and your sense of well-being.

Capturing a widespread desperation, Ann Crittenden, in her *New York Times* review of Brigid Schulte's sobering 2014 book, *Overwhelmed: Work, Love, and Play When No One Has the Time,* allowed that Schulte's sensible solutions were "good suggestions," but then punctuated her review with grim resignation: "But like all self-help advice, they don't measure up against the entrenched forces that are indifferent if not hostile to the emotional well-being of a majority of Americans. Schulte is fighting SEAL Team Six with a pair of fingernail scissors."[1]

This book offers a different view. While I fully agree that we are contending with forces never seen before—and that the modern workplace presents distractions like never before—I also know that any person can learn to modulate distraction and overload well enough to take greater control, while becoming happier, healthier, and more productive in the process. To be sure, as Crittenden, Schulte, and numerous other commentators have shown in well-documented detail, the special forces that oppose a sane and measured life today advance en masse like invisible pincers, nipping at us wherever we turn. And this isn't going to let up. If anything, the number of distractions will continue to grow, exponentially. This is why all the commonly offered advice—such as manage your time and to-do lists more efficiently, multitask better, be more organized—don't and can't work. They're only Band-Aids. Instead, you have to retrain your attention. You have to recognize that the underlying issues of mental distraction—all of which are magnified and even harder to control in the workplace—are within your control. Even if you can't control your environment, you can learn how to reach a more productive mental state of focus, relying on planning, preparation, and technique instead of the frantic efforts people typically use to control their time and attention.

Before you think it can't be done, look at Tim Armstrong, CEO of AOL, the man responsible for turning that company around. To combat "nano-thinking disease," he is in the process of testing a policy at AOL he calls "10% Think Time," which mandates that all executives spend at least four hours a week engaged in an obsolescent activity called *thinking*. Armstrong told me, "It's been a total game-changer for me and for AOL. The companies that take this seriously will have a major strategic advantage in the years to come."[2]

Our current problem, the ongoing mental traffic jam—if not gridlock—in which it's *always* rush hour, grew out of our most spectacular successes, the amazing inventions that define our era. We created the labor-saving devices that catalyzed the unplanned explosion within which we live today. But as Armstrong and enlightened managers everywhere are learning, we can learn to manage what we created. When we learn how to take back controls that we've given away, we can get better at managing our attention and not surrendering it to every distraction.

This book will show you how to focus and be more productive at work. In part I, I'll cover the six most common ways in which people surrender their attention at work, and provide targeted solutions for dealing with each one. Then, in part II, I'll provide an overall plan for managing and training your attention over time so that you are more prepared and more mentally fit to deal with whatever distractions come your way.

But first, let me tell you why I am in an excellent position to show you how to overcome today's attention deficit problem.

attention deficit trait

I'm a focus doctor. An MD, now sixty-four years old as I write these words, I've studied attention and productivity for my entire career. "Attention deficit trait," or ADT, is a term I coined in 1994 to describe what I observed at that time to be an increasingly common problem in the modern workplace. Because I am a specialist in attention deficit disorder (ADD), many men and women seek consultation with me, wondering whether they have some form of attention deficit disorder or attention deficit hyperactivity disorder (ADHD).[3] They come to see me because they've lost their ability to focus on anything; they're always in a rush, bouncing from task to task like boats against the current, worried that they're falling behind even as they strive to get ahead. Multitasking, hopping from project to project, e-mailing while talking on the phone, rushing from meeting to meeting, texting under the table, squeezing in one last call while frantically trying to get to the next appointment on time, ending the day with a frustrated feeling of neither fulfilling all of their goals nor performing at their best, let alone with equanimity, these people look *as if* they have true attention deficit disorder, when, in fact, most of the time, they do not. Instead, most of these people have a severe case of modern life—what I came to call attention deficit trait, or ADT.

ADT differs from ADD or ADHD in that it is caused by the context in which it occurs, while true ADD or ADHD are genetic in origin. That means ADT comes and goes: you may have it during the week, but not on weekends or on vacation; or you may have it when you are in a certain work setting or when interacting with some people but not others. Because people develop ADT in an effort to cope with the stresses in their lives, and because the symptoms actually help them in the short term, the symptoms are "sticky" and may solidify into firm habits, even when life slows and becomes less stressful.

As I saw more and more cases of ADT, I wrote about the problem in an article in the *Harvard Business Review* called "Overloaded Circuits: Why Smart People Underperform." As I discussed in that article and a subsequent book, *CrazyBusy: Overstretched, Overbooked, and About to Snap!*, ADT originates externally, like a virus. It then penetrates into a person's life via the senses and then the brain. It is brought on by the incessant demands, temptations, and opportunities that hijack our attention, filling our heads with a cacophony of mental noise. As our minds fill with such noise—spasmodic synaptic snaps signifying nothing—the brain loses its ability to attend fully and thoughtfully to *anything.*

The symptoms of ADT gradually take over a person. The sufferer doesn't experience a single crisis. The individual doesn't say, "It started the day my boss went crazy," or "It happened the day of the merger," or even, "It started when I got my iPhone." Like dementia, the onset of ADT is far more subtle and insidious. The average worker suffers a series of minor annoyances, finds memory more of a problem than ever, notices the workday becoming ever more unpredictable but definitely longer, and finds it harder and harder to keep up. Not aware how profoundly the circumstances of her life are changing, she does what she always does. She soldiers on. She takes responsibility. She "sucks it up" and doesn't complain even as her workload morphs into a monster she can't manage.

For a grim illustration, imagine the anecdote of the boiled frog: if you take that frog and drop it into boiling water, it will try like mad to jump out. But if you put that same frog into a pot of cold water and gradually turn up the heat, you'll end up with a boiled frog. For most of us, the heat got turned up by the advent of the internet, by the shrinking number of people holding assistant positions, and by the corporate focus on efficiency and productivity, regardless of the human cost.

Fate gave me a catbird seat from which to observe the growing epidemic of ADT that we are experiencing today. I've witnessed the vaporization of attention, as if it were boiling away, while people tried valiantly to keep track of more data than even the most adept human brain could possibly accommodate. Since modern life induces ADT, you may wake up in the morning without it, but by 10 a.m. have developed many of the symptoms, which include the following:

- A heightened distractibility and a persistent feeling of being rushed or in a hurry, even when there's no need to be, combined with a mounting feeling of how superficial your life has become: lots to do, but no depth of thought or feeling.

- An inability to sustain lengthy and full attention to a thought, a conversation, an image, a paragraph, a diagram, a sunset—or anything else, even when you try to.

- A growing tendency toward impatience, boredom, dissatisfaction, restlessness, irritability, frustration, or frenzy, sometimes approaching panic.

- A tendency to hop from task to task, idea to idea, even place to place.

- A tendency to make decisions impulsively, rather than reflecting and taking time to think them through.

- An increasing tendency to avoid thinking altogether, as if it were a luxury you don't have time for.

- A tendency to put off difficult work or conversations, coupled with a tendency to overfill your day with feckless busywork.

- A tendency to feel overwhelmed, even when, in reality, you're not.

- Haunting feelings of guilt about incomplete tasks, coupled with resentment that the tasks were imposed in the first place.

- Difficulty in fully enjoying pleasant moments and genuine achievements.

- Too often saying to yourself, "I'm working really hard but I'm not getting to where I want to be," both at work and in relationships.

- A feeling of loss of control over your own life and a nagging feeling of "What am I missing?"

- A recurring thought that "Someday I will make time for what really matters, but I don't have time to do that today."

- A growing, compulsive need for frequent electronic "hits," for example, checking e-mails, speaking on your iPhone, sending or receiving texts, Googling random subjects, visiting favorite web-sites, or playing games, coupled with almost an addict's yen for them when they are unavailable.

- A tendency to overcommit, make yourself too available, allow too many interruptions, and say yes too quickly.

If you see yourself in many or all of these feelings and tendencies, wel-come to modern life. ADT is everywhere, especially at work.

Consider some of the pernicious effects of ADT. It leads you to respond to others in ways you otherwise wouldn't. How often do you find yourself tuning out when someone—say, a colleague or a friend—tells a long, albeit amusing, anecdote or who poignantly pours his or her heart out, while you fake full attention? Sometimes you might hear yourself responding rudely to a person who is trying to explain an important matter to you. How often do you find yourself just saying "Bottom line it" or "Give me the elevator pitch"?

Hyper-speed makes it impossible for you to absorb what's new or different. So instead of finding new material to help you think in unexpected ways, you start thinking in bite-sized, convenient, mundane chunks made up of what's familiar: the stereotypes, slogans, and buzzwords that trigger stock responses and come to define your predictable, prefabricated beliefs, understandings, and convictions.

the price of ADT

As we all know only too well, the problem has grown more pervasive and severe, costing organizations hundreds of billions of dollars every year and individuals their joie de vivre, if not sanity itself. The biggest price we pay for surrendering our attention is productivity at work. Estimates of the loss of productivity in the workplace due to screen sucking, time wasted online or in front of a screen, as well as other distractions vary widely, but all are in big numbers. A study published in *Inc.* magazine in 2006 estimated that $282 billion was lost annually in the United States to screen sucking. (The estimate was based on a study that showed the average worker spent about two hours—1.86 hours, to be exact—of every eight hours at work wasting time, 52 percent of which was spent "surfing the Internet." The total bill for the wasted time was $544 billion, 52 percent of which equals $282 billion.)[4]

There is actually a nonprofit organization comprising practitioners, researchers, consultants, and other professionals devoted to the problem of information overload, the Information Overload Research Group (IORG; IORGforum.org). According to its website, information overload wastes 25 percent of information workers' time, costing the US economy alone $997 billion annually.[5]

These estimates vary greatly, but there can be no doubt that the real number is huge, and the waste of time and money is mostly preventable.

Another more subtle serpent called "multitasking" seduces millions of us into sabotaging our productivity. While most of us believe that we can get more done by doing two things at once, the proven fact—as documented as long ago as 1995 by cognitive psychologists Robert Rogers and Stephen Monsell—is that switching attention from one task to the other in rapid succession, which is what multitasking actually is, reduces accuracy, increases errors, and diminishes the quality of the work, whatever it may be.[6]

Of course, the cost goes deeper than lost productivity. Imagine ADT in an operating room. Consider this e-mail I recently received from a doctor in charge of training surgeons:

> I supervise attending urologic and transplant surgeons and am a residency program director and try to articulate and create an environment where good decisions are fostered and made in the course of the surgeons' workday (both in and out of the OR). I found your description of ADT and the brain's "survival mode" to seem to have application to decision making in surgery and in daily medical practice. It is my observation that surgeons in the OR typically are handling multiple inputs (pagers, phones, nurses, anesthesia, pressure from delays in a long schedule etc....) and face considerable distraction while they are doing surgery. This, in my opinion, is a set up for "acute ADT" in the OR. It is particularly a problem when things are not going

as planned or expected in the operation and when the situation demands executive cognitive function, creativity, and mental freshness. It is interesting that with all of the attention directed to making the OR safer, there has been little attention directed to focus on the patient and the operation during the operative event.[7]

As José Ortega y Gasset wrote in a much different time, "Every destiny is dramatic, tragic in its deepest meaning. Whoever has not felt the danger of our times palpitating under his hand, has not really penetrated to the vitals of destiny, he has merely pricked its surface."[8] The surface of *our* age has grown vaster and more unavoidable than when Ortega wrote in 1930; we all face far greater risk now of only pricking the surface, missing the vitals of life altogether.

The modern danger is that we grow so engrossed with and seduced by what matters so little, busy with and ruled by whatever presses upon us, that we overlook and thereby destroy our most important projects and goals through neglect.

prescription for focus

Although I never planned to when I was in medical school or residency, over the past thirty-plus years, I've turned focus and attention into my specialty, a specialty that didn't exist when I was in training, but is booming now. If you search for the word "focus" on Amazon.com, you will get 463,374 titles, including Daniel Goleman's 2013 book, *Focus: The Hidden Driver of Excellence*.[9] While this book gives an excellent account of why focus is important to achieving goals, it doesn't look at the many ways people lose their ability to focus at work or provide practical solutions for training the attention and regaining control at work.

Most people don't see lack of focus as the root of their problem or even as a possibility. Most of those who consult me simply blame themselves for their failure to be happier or more successful. They don't make excuses or blame the system or a difficult boss. "Maybe I'm just a born underachiever," they conclude, or "Maybe I just don't have what it takes to get where I want to get to." They are worried about their jobs, their relationships, and their families, but they only blame themselves in response to the problems they face.

People are usually in more pain than they let on. If they even recognize how much their problem relates to impaired focus, they deal with it simply by trying to overpower it. But that's like trying to cure nearsightedness by squinting harder. Ironically, the harder they try, the more likely they are to fail, which leads them to blame themselves even more, thus intensifying the problem. They don't need to work harder, just smarter.

This book will teach you to work smarter, not harder. First, by recognizing and dealing with the six most common distractions or patterns of ADT at work, and second, by learning a new set of techniques for managing your attention over time, you'll be equipped to overcome whatever distraction is holding you back from doing your best work.

the six most common distractions at work—and how to overcome them

Imagine if you could work with the same kind of focus you did ten, fifteen, or twenty years ago, before the deluge. Imagine if you could repel the tsunami of distractions, interruptions, and sudden changes that buffet you all the time. Imagine if you could control your mind and your work environment so well that you get super-focused often and regularly produce work on a par with your best ever. Imagine coming to work eager to get onto a project, and confident that you'll get it done well. Imagine living without daily frenzy, frustration, fear, and fizzle. Imagine regaining control over your thinking and emotions, surpassing your best regularly, breaking new ground confidently, and feeling in charge, rather than at the mercy of our unpredictable world. That's exactly what I can help you do.

In part I, I start with the six most common varieties of ADT through which people lose focus at work including one case of true, full-blown ADHD. I show what each syndrome looks like and give practical tools and advice for addressing each. The people I describe in these chapters are composites of the many I've worked with over my thirty years in practice and share the same kinds of high-pressure lives as most of us. They all obey a brave imperative to keep up with everything at work and at home, to pay the bills, to raise the kids, to do it all, or, as Zorba put it, "the full catastrophe."[10]

Here are thumbnail sketches of the six syndromes I'll cover in sequence, in chapters 1 through 6.

SCREEN SUCKING: How to Control Your Electronics So They Don't Control You. Our electronic devices, which help us enormously when used properly, have spawned a new kind of addiction in people who feel a high when hyper-focusing on their electronic screens and feel at a loss without them. In this chapter, you'll meet Les, a financial researcher who has lost his ability to think creatively and connect with others, thanks to a screen addiction, driven by deeper feelings of helplessness and loss of control that reach back into his past.

MULTITASKING: How to Say No When You Have More to Do Than Time to Do It. In this chapter I'll paint a picture of Jean, a lawyer who does everything she can to handle an overwhelming load. Facing a daily onslaught of tasks, people like Jean become increasingly and uncharacteristically hurried, curt, peremptory, and unfocused, while trying valiantly to pretend that everything is under control. Jean's problem was amplified by feelings she developed early in life that she needed always to be "good," to do all she was asked to do and more, and to do it all perfectly. No one actually told her she had to be perfect; she put that burden on herself, feeling it was the best way to feel good about herself and about life.

IDEA HOPPING: How to Finish What You Start. The old woman who lived in a shoe, as the nursery rhyme goes, had so many children she didn't know what to do. Like Ashley, whom you will meet in this chapter, some particularly creative, entrepreneurial professionals may have many brainchildren, but they can't sustain their focus long enough to raise any to maturity. In Ashley's case, the issue ran deeper because her competitive mother ridiculed Ashley's childhood achievements, leaving her with a lifelong feeling that to succeed meant to encounter danger and rejection.

WORRYING: How to Turn Toxic Worry into Problem Solving. Many people waste chunks of each day attending to something other than what they want to be attending to, often in response to feelings of anxiety. In this chapter, I'll introduce Jack, a financially successful but incessantly worried executive who carries childhood patterns of fear and anxiety into adulthood in ways that damage his health and prevent him from making the most of his career and having a good relationship with his wife and children.

PLAYING THE HERO: How to Stop Fixing Everyone's Problems—Except Your Own. Like many professionals who sabotage themselves by placing the needs of others above their own, Mary also has a knack for carrying the negative water of the organization. The late professor Peter Frost of the University of British Columbia described such people as heroic toxic handlers who hold the organization together while sacrificing themselves in the process. Mary learned this role early, as a child protecting the rest of the family from a narcissistic tyrant of a father.

DROPPING THE BALL: How to Stop Underachieving at Work.
Some people suffer from an undiagnosed condition, true ADHD
rather than ADT, which causes them to underachieve through
an inability to get organized. Like Sharon, their mental focus
is clouded by the external chaos and clutter within which they
work—the piles, the scattered papers and other materials,
the lists, the journals, memos and other missives, not to mention memorabilia, that accrue every day at home and at work.
Sharon's problem was exacerbated by the fact she'd developed
the habit of blaming herself early on in her life, being intensely
self-critical and feeling obliged to be good at what she was
bad at rather than pursuing the activities she loved and had
talent in.

In each chapter, I combine general, practical tips and suggestions with
advice rooted in a person's individual psychology. I try to zero in on the
emotions involved, not just peruse the details of the chaos. And I try to
leave you with tips and takeaways you can use to combat each one of
these syndromes.

training your attention—how to manage and maintain your ability to focus

In part II, chapters 7 through 13, I present the elements of a broad basic
plan for managing your attention more generally, with techniques for
developing habits to help you consistently find focus and achieve your
goals. I provide examples and offer specific tips as the book unfolds. Here
are its bones, bared:

ENERGY. You—especially your brain—can't focus without
energy, and plenty of it. As your supply of energy gets low, you

start to fade. Taking steps to monitor your brain's energy supply is as basic and essential as keeping your car's tank full of gas. Most people ignore or take for granted this fundamental necessity, as if the supply was infinite, and they do not monitor carefully how they spend their energy, thus wasting great quantities of it on trivial tasks. But when you invest your energy wisely and see to it that energy tank is always full, you become able to feel positive emotion.

EMOTION. Emotion is the on-off switch for learning and for peak performance. Often ignored or taken for granted, your emotional state drives the quality of your focus and thus the results you can achieve. If you work in a fear-driven organization that is low on trust, your performance will necessarily suffer. It's a neurological fact. But if you work in a group that is high on trust and low on fear, then you can achieve at your best. The better you understand yourself, your personal psychology, and your emotional hot buttons, the better able you will be to hold yourself in the right emotional state for focus, while steering clear of the negative states that render sharp focus impossible. Positive emotion, in turn, galvanizes engagement.

ENGAGEMENT. You must be interested in order to pay close attention. You must also be motivated. Interest and motivation equal engagement. Such engagement develops naturally when you work in your "sweet spot," the overlap of three spheres: what you love to do, what you are very good at doing, and what advances the mission of the group or what someone will pay you to do. In addition, there should be some novelty in what you're doing and some room for creative input on your part to hold your attention. Lack of novelty leads to boredom, which leads to loss of focus. But beware, too much novelty and too much creative input will cause you to wander all over and grow confused, which is why you also need structure.

STRUCTURE. Such a simple word, but such a magnificent tool when used creatively and wisely. Armstrong's "10% Think Time" is a perfect example of structure. Structure refers to how you shape your day, how you spend your time, what boundaries you create, what rules you follow, which assistants you employ, what filing system you use, what hours you keep, what breaks you take, what priorities you set up, which tasks you take on and which you farm out, what plans you make, and what flexibility you create. Without structure, focus is impossible. Chaos reigns. In order to create, preserve, and promote your own best structures, you need to take control.

CONTROL. In today's world, if you don't take your time, it will be taken from you. Most people exert less control over how they use their time than they should. Take back control. The fact is, most people give away great gobs of their time and attention every day without meaning to and usually without being aware that they are. They surrender their attention to the onslaught of modern life without putting up much of a fight, as if they were overmatched. No one would dump $150 into the garbage every day, but most of us flush at least a hundred fifty minutes every day without even noticing we're doing it.

These five elements—energy, emotion, engagement, structure, and control—combine to create a plan that will allow you to perform at your best without feeling frazzled, frantic, and feckless. As I will show in chapters 7 through 13, you need to individualize your own plan, based on your situation and your own personality and emotional makeup, but the basic elements of this plan will work for everyone.

Each of the six syndromes found in chapters 1 through 6 illustrates one person's struggle to focus. You will likely see some of yourself in a few, even a bit of yourself in all of them. To help you sort out where you should put most of your efforts, I created an assessment, which can be found at hbr.org/assessments/adt. This will give you a weighted score, showing you which of the syndromes most apply to you. With this knowledge in hand, this book will help you get started on combating the distractions you most commonly deal with and developing your plan to regain focus at work.

the six most common distractions at work—and how to overcome them

screen sucking

how to control your electronics so they don't control you

Les Marshall stared at the computer screen he always had set at eye level as he typed, fluently, effortlessly, almost as if on automatic pilot, like a pianist playing a piece he's played a thousand times before. He displayed no emotion, and other than the movement of his fingers, he showed no movement other than an ever so slight rocking back and forth of his upper body.

His browser was open to several windows at once. One was open to Morningstar.com, where Les could look up the latest earnings and trend information that he needed to produce his report. Another was open to a blog on *Huffington Post*, another to ESPN.com, and a fourth to eBay, where Les could browse and shop for the Harley motorcycle gear, art deco lamps, kitchen tools, and other stuff he amused himself with.

Of course, there was the window open to Mrskin.com, where Les could ogle nude photos of lovely celebrity women or watch clips from the more explicit parts of recent movies. But he'd shifted from sex to food, thinking about picking up groceries for dinner after work, so he'd checked out Cooksillustrated.com as well. Since he and his wife were trying to conceive a child, yet another screen was open to a fertility calendar that she had told him about.

In fact, all the stray thoughts that he'd had during the day seemed to be open to their own website, as the browser history noted. Meanwhile, his e-mail dinged and his iPhone pinged with every message. Like eager puppies, they, too, begged for his attention.

When Les worked on a report, he was on automatic pilot. In copying and pasting text and numbers into the familiar format, Les worked without pause. Not only did he know his keyboard so well that he never had to look down at it, he never even needed to stop and think. Since his doctor had told him the straight-on eye-to-screen angle was orthopedically preferable to looking downward, head erect had become his permanent posture at work.

His boss, Carl, would walk by sometimes and look in on him. Les worked with his door open unless he was in a private discussion, but since the back of Les's monitor faced the door, Carl couldn't see what Les was looking at. "Les, I can never tell if you are working or daydreaming," he'd say to him.

"Look at my fingers, Carl," Les would reply, somewhat defensively. "You can see them under the monitor. My fingers are always moving. That should prove to you I'm always working."

"No, you misunderstand me," Carl would say. "Sometimes I wish you would *stop* moving those fingers for a minute and just sit and think more about new companies we should be investing in. You used to do a lot more of that. Thinking is work, and you're a very smart man. We could really use your thoughts."

"Okay, Carl, I'll give it a try," Les would say, while thinking to himself, sure, he wants me to think, just as long as I still get done the

People who fit the category of ADT outlined in this chapter tend to agree with the following statements.

If my cellphone is out of reach, I feel distressed.

I can waste an hour online without even knowing it.

I have more to do than time to do it.

I lack discipline.

I secretly go online at work and at home.

I often retreat into the cyber world when stressed at work.

I can't imagine not taking my smartphone with me to lunch.

I always want more.

I underachieve at work.

I have the will; I just haven't found the way.

mountain of work I don't have time to get done even without wasting time thinking.

As a research analyst in an investment firm, Les was paid primarily to ferret out the data on companies his superiors were interested in. He was handsomely rewarded for delivering the famously well-hewn data summaries he so regularly and punctually produced. However, over the past several years and most especially in the past six months, Les had noted a gradual but by now unmistakable change within himself. He felt himself becoming what he called "stupid." He felt he'd lost whatever flair for coming up with investment ideas he might once have had. No one had detected it as yet, except him. But he couldn't deny it, as much as he tried to. He couldn't help but notice the emptiness within himself now and again.

It was as if all the data he lived in and with while writing his reports was polluting his mind, like so many toxic molecules, killing his curiosity, wit, and spunk, leaving him to wake each day into an increasingly drab and silent mental spring. But when he was busying himself with reports, there was plenty of action. That action was a camouflage: lots of movement of fingers, eyes, and even synapses. The repetitive movement of fingers aligned with the repetitive patterns of his thoughts were all stimulating, in the sense that the electrical activity of his brain never waned, but none of it was original or deep. He was stalled in fast-revving mental neutral. He took on nothing difficult. He suffered no pain. He saw no gain.

While Les could see the difference between himself now and his old self of just a few years ago, his ability to observe himself accurately was waning. Instead, his mind was being sucked into cyberspace, enchanted by the ubiquitous, beckoning siren of the web. He embraced this force that was taking him over with a kind of narcoleptic surrender.

Dozens of screens linked to the Google universe nearly always took the center stage of his attention. Screens became octopod extensions of his body. They were eye level at his desk at work, cupped in his hand on the subway, sitting next to his fork at the dinner table, hooked to his pants when he was walking or jogging, and resting on his bedside table as he went to sleep. Never was he far from them.

lights on, but nobody home

Now forty-two years old and married to Lyn, whom he'd met at work, Les knew he was in jeopardy, teetering between being all right and tumbling into an abyss. Soon, he would fall one way or the other. He barely knew *how* he realized he was in danger, but a fading voice, like an old coach cheering him on from a distant sideline of his life, would interrupt him now and then and try to get his attention, saying, *Les, you're losing your chance at the life you want; you're losing your dream. Get a grip.*

But the voice would soon get drowned out by all the work there was to do. How could he ignore the work? If he were rich, he could pursue dreams, consider the meaning of life, and heed that inner voice, but since he was far from rich, he had to get the work done that he got paid to do. Pursuing dreams or pondering meaning was not work he got paid to do.

"I have to be practical," he said to Lyn. "If we are going to live here and if we are going to have a baby, I have to be practical."

"You're not being practical, Les," Lyn replied. "You're just escaping. You're never with me. You're in love with your laptop. You're in a trance that just grows and grows."

"My work happens to depend upon electronics and the internet. You know that."

"I could be sitting here stark naked," Lyn said, "and you wouldn't notice. That's not normal."

"Of course I'd notice, honey. I love you. You're the sexiest girl I know," Les said, tentatively reaching out a hand, which Lyn did not take.

"I don't know whether to laugh or cry," she said. "As for a baby, unless Immaculate Conception makes a comeback, we're gonna lose out on that, too."

"I'm sorry," Les said. "I know I've been preoccupied lately."

"The sad part," Lyn replied, "is that you've been preoccupied for years and you haven't even known it."

But he had known it. When that voice would speak up, that inner coach from the past, on his way to sleep, in the shower, at an odd off-guard moment, he'd feel a shiver, as if arrested by Officer Truth for a moment. But, rather than heed the warning, he'd quickly rush into the demands of the day, the practical agenda he followed ostensibly in order to keep Lyn's and his life afloat.

Without knowing what he was doing, he developed more and more of a habit, then a compulsion, always to be online in front of a screen. If he were denied access to his e-mail for even a minute or two, he would feel an itch, an irritable yearning for a hit, a hit of e-mail, as absurd as that might sound. He knew it, but he kept on denying it enough that he didn't have to do anything about it. Instead, using the rationale of needing to keep up, he glued himself ever more to screens, so that even in the bathroom or in meetings, he'd be texting or surfing. He developed clever and subtle means of concealing his activity from others, lest he be thought rude. He also developed an uncanny skill of being able to respond to a question, even when he had heard none of it.

For example, in a meeting, he would simply hear his name, "Les." Taking that as his cue, he would offer up any number of stock phrases that were sure to cover his mental disappearance. He might say, "I think we ought to get more input," or, "I like the tone of this discussion so far. We are really working as a team, even though some people might not see it," or, "There's no harm in looking at both sides." His favorite was, "I was just thinking about the idea we discussed last week. Can we go back to that?" He liked this one because it allowed him to admit he'd missed what was going on, but he'd missed it in the service of a good purpose.

The more he interacted with screens, the less he interacted with live humans. After a while, he noticed that humans annoyed him more than they used to. They could not be controlled, they were rude, they disagreed, they were selfish, and so on. He also noticed that he enjoyed more and more the comfort and stimulation of the electronic world. While he rarely played games—that was a field he had yet to plow—electronic existence felt like an upgrade on regular life. In screen-land, he could be in control. He could be stimulated all the time. He was never bored. Best of all, he could get paid for it.

What a bonanza this electronic world offered. Les somehow thought it would save him and allow him to realize all his dreams. It was bitterly paradoxical that this bonanza, Les's method of saving himself, was actually destroying him, his marriage, and all his dreams slowly, day by day. He was getting sucked down by an electronic field.

Lyn warned him of the danger he was in; Carl did as well. Carl, in fact, meant it when he urged Les to spend more time thinking. Carl valued Les's creative powers, far more, as it turned out, than Les did. Les would have loved to believe both Lyn and Carl, and achieve the greatness he felt he had in him. But such was the power of Les's insidiously mounting compulsion that he denied the validity of Lyn's and Carl's objections.

Les's addiction

Les's form of ADT—a growing compulsion to be online, causing him to lose focus on everything else—is the fastest-growing type of ADT in today's world. Once a joke, compulsive use of electronics has become a serious and widespread problem. It is the newest addiction, and, like all addictions, in its severest forms can lead to tragic consequences.

Having worked with many addicts of all kinds in my career, I've found that *the* most poorly recognized fact about this group of people is how enormously gifted most of them truly are. Addicts have been doing what Les was doing—gradually self-destructing—for thousands of years. It is far more the rule than the exception to find ability, drive, and even genius or remarkable talent buried beneath the addiction, whatever that addiction might be. Society typically inflicts its harshest, most contemptuous scorn on addicts, adding shame to the heap of obstacles they face. But if they do manage to gain control of their addiction, they commonly go on to marvelously contribute to the world.

Because it is a new problem, Les's particular addiction is usually missed or not even considered an addiction. His denial of what was going on—even though a part of him knew all too well what that was—is one of the chief reasons addicts never get the help they need.

Denial is the most common trick addicts play on themselves to justify continuing their addiction. Since electronics are essential for most people's work, we don't associate them with the psychology of an addict. Yet addiction was precisely the trap Les was falling into. If he'd been able to reflect on his own past, he'd remember that both his parents, while not full-blown alcoholics, struggled to control their drinking and subjected Les to many embarrassing scenes he'd just as soon forget. He'd also remember that he himself smoked cigarettes in college and was able to quit only because the social pressure to do so became so intense. He'd recognize that he was genetically wired to be vulnerable to compulsive and addictive activities of all kinds, from substances and sex to spending and gambling and, yes, to electronics. The predisposition to addiction of all kinds resides in your genetic endowment.

There are many forms of digital addiction or self-destructive digital habits. Here are just a few, all taken from the news or from my practice:

- A student is so attached to video games that he cannot get homework done or study for tests, and he is flunking out.

- During meetings, a woman sneaks onto websites on her smartphone so she can shop. She not only endangers her job, but runs up credit card debt that threatens both her marriage and her financial solvency.

- Internet sex sites so preoccupy a man that he loses his job and his marriage.

- A woman develops a cyber affair with a man she met in a chat room and about whom she doesn't care, and in so doing brings her marriage to a crashing halt.

- A man gets fired from his job after repeated warnings not to spend so much time on his iPhone.

Like everyone else, from spouses to parents to bosses to flight attendants, doctors (like me) wrestle with the issue of what to do about electronic addiction. Now that we've discovered this new fire, what are we to do with the Promethean problem we've set loose upon the world?

Since this form of addiction has no precedent, we cannot look to the past to guide us in exact detail. But we can take from the past some general advice about addictions or bad habits. We can also learn to temper our alarm with the awareness that all change and every new technology has been greeted with fear and the wringing of hands. For example, when trains first became a common means of human transportation, newspaper articles deplored the likely epidemic of brain damage the swaying movements of the train would cause. When telephone service became widespread, experts predicted an epidemic of brain tumors as well as an inability to speak face-to-face. And we still hear shrill choruses deploring the watching of television, deeming TV an "idiot box" that will inexorably render us and our children mentally slow, if not demented.

While taking care not to overreact like alarmists or Luddites, we also can't ignore what has become, in a few short years and spreading faster than kudzu, a massive problem all made possible by the new technologies that have insinuated themselves into every minute of our daily lives. Of course, the problems caused by screen sucking are also balanced by much good. Our electronic devices help us everywhere, every day, in a multitude of ways. They helped runners and visitors at the Boston Marathon find places to stay the night following a bombing. They help poor people in India connect with important information about health, water, and food; they help people who suffer under dictators to break free. Indeed, a person's *inability* to use them can be economically and socially crippling in today's world. Just as fire became a huge force for good and ill, so have our electronics. While the upside is obvious, the downside is perhaps less easy to perceive (see table 1-1 for their beneficial and problematic aspects).

TABLE 1-1

Beneficial and problematic aspects of electronic devices

Beneficial	Problematic
Instantaneous communication via voice, text, video, or photo with capacity to copy millions at once if so desired	Interruptions and excessive cc'ing
Quick send-and-response time	Impulsiveness
Portable, can be used anywhere	Rudeness and offensiveness
Instant access to everything ever known or thought	Too much information available, information not reliable or screened
Portable entertainment device	Habit forming, even addicting
Access to people worldwide, 24/7/365	"Electronic moment" replaces "human moment"
Private	Illusion of privacy; conversations can be monitored or hacked
Speed	With speed comes superficiality
Huge volume of data	Too much data, too little thinking
Screen can promote focus	Hypnotic time waster

what exactly is screen addiction?

You might become a habitual watcher of television or listen to radio for hours on end, but those are a one-way stream; you absorb what the broadcast sends you, but you don't broadcast back. Our digital devices, on the other hand, are two way; we join the online world in ways that we can't with radio or television. The internet allows us to live in a digital universe where we can do everything from start a business to fall in love. We can buy and sell, chat, seduce, interview, plan a garden, set up a marriage, buy a house, find a spouse, get an advanced degree, or mount a political campaign.

It's easy to get hooked on certain online activities. Hundreds of websites exactly resemble a casino onscreen. You put down your credit card, and, and, voilà, you're in your own private Las Vegas. You can win or lose just as much, just as fast. Dopamine floods your brain, just as it would in a real casino. You can do the same with sex, online shopping, and just about any addictive or compulsive activity that does not require your actual, physical presence.

The situation gets even dicier. A person can develop an addiction, as Les did, without falling prey to any of the well-known addictive activities like gambling, sex, or spending. A person can simply become addicted to the *feeling* of being online. Biologically speaking, the same dopamine circuitry that is activated in traditional addictions now is activated simply by spending too much time online.

I've interviewed many people with this problem. They talk of their need to be online because it gives them a freewheeling state of mind where anything goes and nothing is shut down. They talk about craving it when they can't have it and about feeling irritable and jittery on flights that don't offer Wi-Fi. They admit to losing relationships and jobs due to their inability to control their craving. They describe the feeling of being online as a kind of anesthesia that eases the pain of everyday life.

What are we to do? Before developing solutions to this problem, we need to name it. We need a framework of understanding and a vocabulary to guide us through what we've gotten ourselves into.

No group has standardized a procedure for dealing with the use of electronic devices more effectively than, oddly enough, the airlines. They've been on the case for years. That now leaves the rest of us to figure out what our policies and procedures ought to be. In dealing with screen addiction, the inexperienced must lead the even less experienced. Since we don't know what to call the phenomenon of excessive or inappropriate use of electronic devices, we don't know how to talk about it very well. We don't even know how much use is excessive or precisely what is inappropriate.

A decade ago, former Microsoft executive Linda Stone observed that people paid "continuous partial attention" to just about everything.[1]

We are always scanning for opportunities—for the next excitement, the next hit, the next twinge of happiness or anger from good news or bad, whatever wandering digital image or thought that lights up the various corners of our brains. We're glued to our screens because, like gamblers, we want to see what comes up on the next roll of the screen dice.

Since Stone first offered that observation, the problem of continuous partial attention has ballooned into one of the signal (pun intended) difficulties of our time. The new condition characterized by the misuse of electronic devices has acquired various names assigned by various groups. These include problematic computer use (PCU), computer addiction (CA), communication addiction disorder (CAD), and internet addiction (IA). Then there's term the psychiatric profession's new diagnostic manual, the DSM-5, first came up with—internet use disorder, which went by the unfortunate acronym IUD. Later, the definition was narrowed and the name changed to internet gaming disorder. It is not an official diagnosis, but rather is listed in the section of the DSM-5 called "Conditions for Further Study." Here's how the DSM-5 defines internet gaming disorder:

> Persistent and recurrent use of the Internet to engage in games, often with other players, leading to clinically significant impairment or distress as indicated by five (or more) of the following in a 12-month period:
>
> 1. Preoccupation with Internet games. (The individual thinks about previous gaming activity or anticipates playing the next game; Internet gaming becomes the dominant activity in daily life.)
>
>   Note: This disorder is distinct from Internet gambling, which is included under gambling disorder.
>
> 2. Withdrawal symptoms when Internet gaming is taken away. (These symptoms are typically described as

irritability, anxiety, or sadness, but there are no physical signs of pharmacological withdrawal.)

3. Tolerance: the need to spend increasing amounts of time engaged in Internet games.

4. Unsuccessful attempts to control the participation in Internet games.

5. Loss of interests in previous hobbies and entertainment as a result of, and with the exception of, Internet games.

6. Continued excessive use of Internet games despite knowledge of negative psychosocial problems.

7. Has deceived family members, therapists, or others regarding the amount of Internet gaming.

8. Use of the Internet games to escape or relieve a negative mood (e.g., feelings of helplessness, guilt, anxiety).

9. Has jeopardized or lost a significant relationship, job, or educational or career opportunity because of participation in Internet games.

   Note: Only non-gambling Internet games are included in this disorder. Use of the Internet for required activities in a business or profession is not included; nor is the disorder intended to include other recreational or social Internet use. Similarly, sexual Internet sites are excluded.

Specify current severity:

Internet gaming disorder can be mild, moderate, or severe depending on the degree of disruption of normal activities. Individuals with less severe Internet gaming disorder may exhibit fewer symptoms and less disruption of their lives. Those with severe Internet gaming disorder will have more hours spent on the computer and more severe loss of relationships or career or school opportunities.[2]

I find the DSM-5 description too narrow, as the problem extends far beyond just gaming. I choose to call the syndrome by the broadest and most inclusive term I can think of: problematic use of electronic devices (PUED), thereby covering the widest ground possible. In my classification, the use of any electronic device for communication, learning, business, entertainment, or anything else *that causes a serious behavioral problem as perceived by the user or any other person or group* might be considered worthy of diagnosis and treatment by a medical or mental health professional. I leave the term intentionally ambiguous and vague, because we're in vague and ambiguous territory. What's normal in one setting—say, the office of a trader on the commodities exchange—would be excessive in the waiting area of a funeral parlor. As I've noted, we have no universally accepted social norms. For some passengers, someone speaking on his cellphone on the commuter rail may be fine; for others, it may be beyond the pale. Answering a cellphone during dinner may be no problem for one spouse, but grounds for a big argument for another. One person's problematic use is another person's normal.

I have classified PUED into five levels (see table 1-2). Les had reached level five, the addictive level. He needed help. He dimly recognized that he was in trouble, but some kind of outside intervention would be his best source for recovery. It may sound strange, even alarmist, to apply terms like "recovery" and "addiction" to the use of electronics, our era's great and defining gift. Yet, we are now at a stage where these wonderful tools can and often do impair and even ruin lives. Fortunately, there is reliable help for Les and others like him. It is not as difficult to overcome the problematic use of electronics as it is to quit smoking or control drinking. In this case, what is needed is not abstinence. Few people can live in today's world without using electronics, so abstinence is not an option.

To fix the problem, Les and others like him should begin by naming the problem and by owning up to its severity. Les fell prey to what used to be a joke—excessive use of electronics—but is a joke no more. It is a fast-growing, major disorder. As is true of all addictions, near-addictions, or

TABLE 1-2

Levels of problematic use of electronic devices (PUED)

PUED level	Symptoms
0. No symptoms	
1. Conflictive	Usage is annoying to at least one other person.
2. Mild	Usage is annoying to others, if not to the user, and does not abate when others urge user to cut back.
3. Moderate	Usage is annoying to others and causing problems in user's personal, educational, or professional life. User may deny or acknowledge problem.
4. Severe	Usage is both annoying to others and demonstrably destructive to user's personal, educational, or professional life. User may deny or acknowledge problem. User feels unable to control problem.
5. Addictive	Not only is usage annoying and demonstrably destructive to user's personal, educational, or professional life, but it rises to the level of addiction, including at least two of six defining characteristics of an addiction: 1. *Salience*—the activity becomes most important activity in user's life. 2. *Mood-modification*—a high, a soothing, or a numbing feeling when using. 3. *Tolerance*—increasing amounts of use needed to get same effect. 4. *Withdrawal*—some or all of the following symptoms occur when usage is denied: craving; irritability; anger; agitation; bargaining; rule or law breaking to gain access; insomnia; waking in middle of night; dreaming of using; inability to focus; somatic symptoms such as headache, indigestion, muscle twitching, pacing, nonspecific musculoskeletal aches and pains, lethargy, stupor. 5. *Conflict*—with others and within self due to usage. 6. *Relapse*—tendency to resume previous maladaptive patterns of usage when allowed access.

bad habits, the first hurdle is to overcome denial. Les doesn't want to give up his "binky"—his electronics—because he's come to prefer his screen life to his real life. That's true of all addicts. The addiction provides a pleasurable state of mind that cannot reliably be found in ordinary life. Despite having a great wife, a job rife with opportunity, and a boss who wanted to help him grow, Les fell back into addiction out of a fundamental lack of faith in himself and a feeling of powerlessness to advance his career.

My job was to challenge Les sufficiently to get his attention, but not so much as to beat him down. He was already beaten down enough. Addicts don't like themselves very much; neither does the world. Indeed, they are among our most despised citizens, scorned by themselves and by society. The trick for me was to replace the moral diagnosis that Les, at some deep level, had attached to himself—namely, "you are bad, weak, undisciplined, and a loser"—and replace it with a morally neutral diagnosis that confers some hope like, "You have important gifts you have yet to unwrap."

I gave with one hand: "You have talent." And I took with the other: "Get off your butt and use that talent." It was great when he got mad at me. Anger is a good spur to action, the first sign a person is emerging from lethargy. But I always had to be careful not to hurt his feelings so much that he'd shut down and withdraw.

As with most addicts, Les possessed far more talent than he realized or used. One reason I like to work with all kinds of addicts is that they have the potential to make great progress once they are out of denial and feel some hope. Addictions of all kinds cost businesses much more than most people realize. Not only do they cause millions of illnesses and deaths, they also cause poor or suboptimal performance in the workplace, which Les's case vividly demonstrates.

The solution is simple, but extremely difficult to enact: turn it off (TIO). Of course, were it that easy, we wouldn't need treatment programs, and addictions (tobacco, alcohol, illicit drugs, sex, food, and gambling) would not be costing some $559 billion per year in the United States.[3]

Were addictions easy or only rather difficult to treat, they wouldn't be costing us countless lives and vast sums of money. The fact is that addictions pose a problem science has not come close to solving. So difficult are additions to treat that we have not yet found a program that consistently achieves even modest success. Alcoholics Anonymous and twelve-step programs, in general, widely recognized as the gold standard in the treatment of addictions, achieve a shockingly low success rate, but their mediocre track record is the best we have. About one in fifteen people who enter AA or other twelve-step programs will be able to become and stay sober, a depressing 5 percent to 10 percent success rate.

That is not to say that I don't recommend AA and twelve-step programs. I do. They're the best standardized programs we have. They start where all treatment ought to start: in human connection. Twelve-step programs replace the drug of abuse with human fellowship, and therein resides the heart of their success.

In working with Les, I prescribed human connection as a replacement for screen time. It was not an easy sell, but the best way to go. From there, I followed a psychological model proposed by Lance Dodes, MD, a retired Harvard Medical School professor who spent his entire professional career helping people who struggled with addiction. He believes that addiction serves to reverse an overwhelming sense of helplessness. The minute the addict *decides* to use—be it alcohol, sex, spending, gambling, or, in Les's case, electronics—the addict feels better. He feels pleasure and relief, just from having made the decision to use. It is not the substance or the activity that brings the pleasure at first, but *the decision to use it*. Making a decision to use replaces a feeling of helplessness with a feeling of control, which confers its benefits even before the substance or the activity enters the system.

Dodes goes on to say that while relieving helplessness is the function of addiction, the driving force behind it is rage at that helplessness, like a prisoner raging at the bars that surround him. So intense is the rage that it overrides sound judgment and self-interest. But rather than feel the rage and express it directly, which could reverse the addiction, the addict shies from that. He uses his drug or activity, rather than feeling his true emotions. As Dodes puts it, "Every addictive act is a substitute for a more direct behavior."[4]

In the context of the human connection Les made with me, we were able to draw out his feelings and find direct expression. He did indeed feel helpless that he could not advance in his career or live up to his expectations or those of others. And he did, indeed, feel rage at this, much as any person perpetually held back feels rage. Once he was able to access those feelings, it became far easier for him to give up what Dr. Edward Khantzian, another giant in the field of addiction research, calls his "self-medicating," and replace that with more constructive expression of feelings so that he came out of his addictive shell.[5]

In dealing with addiction, near-addiction, and maladaptive patterns of using, I recommend a combination of a twelve-step program (there's nothing to lose, there's fellowship to gain, and it's the best standard-ized program out there) as well as the psychological model Dodes espouses. We got lucky because Les came to see me without a lot of prodding. This is unusual for an addict who has not hit bottom and who is not mandated by the court to seek help. He came because he read one of my books and saw himself in it. "I want to check you out," he announced.

If he had not opened the door, he likely would have lost his job and his marriage before seeking help. But fate intervened, so we got a head start. With the collaboration of his wife, Lyn, and his boss, Carl, I was able to set up a plan whereby Les could look at his behavior objectively; get support from a group for people with various kinds of addiction, which I referred him to; and use a daily plan of behavior modification aimed at reducing his screen sucking, while replacing it with activities that used more of his creative faculties.

When I apply the basic plan to treat ADT to Les and others like him who struggle with screen sucking, I note the following dangers associated with each element of the plan:

1. ENERGY. The addiction to electronics drains mental energy like a slow cerebral bleed.

2. EMOTION. When you screen suck, you enter into a kind of trance and are emotionally neutral. You feel no joy, rage, or sorrow. You feel very little.

3. ENGAGEMENT. Feeling so little emotion, your only sense of engagement is with the screen, with the ongoing synaptic stimulation you get, so you disengage with the important tasks, people, and ideas with which you might otherwise be engaged.

4. STRUCTURE. The structure of the electronic device and the systems it connects you with cause you to surrender your attention. This is an example of how structure can work against you. The very force that could be your ally becomes your enemy, with your permission.

5. CONTROL. In addiction—and bad habits in general—you fail to exercise the control you have. At some level you lose that control. That's what intervention aims to do: restore your control.

Most people who contend with the problem of screen sucking do not become addicted, as Les did, or even nearly addicted. Nonetheless, their habit can cause major reductions in their productivity. To help these people, I offer some practical tips for fixing the problem.

WHAT TO DO ABOUT IT

10 tips for reducing screen sucking

---

1 Honestly assess how much time you spend on electronics every day. Most people grossly underestimate this figure. If you can, keep a record of use of electronic devices, an RUED. Just jot down when you log on and off, or record your on and off times in a voice memo.

2 Based on your RUED or estimated RUED, gauge where you could cut back. Don't say you can't cut back. You can. This is likely your largest or nearly largest waste of time, so don't squander a good chance to reclaim the time you've surrendered.

3 Create pockets in your day reserved for screen time. A half hour in the morning, a half hour in the afternoon—whatever works for you. Outside those pockets, turn it off. Have an assistant notify you if you are urgently needed. Make your coworkers and customers aware that you may not be available at all times.

4 Turn off your devices during social engagements, like luncheons and coffee breaks.

5 When you get bored, don't use your electronic device like a binky. Do something more productive when you are bored. Read an article you've been meaning to read. Or call an associate you've been meaning to contact. Or write the difficult memo you've been putting off.

6 Keep a list in your notes (wherever you store notes) of things to do when bored, other than screen suck.

7 Avoid addictive or habit-forming websites and games. You know which ones they are for you. Once you get out of the habit of visiting them, they will fade into the oblivion they ought to occupy.

8 Encourage your group or division where you work to collaborate on creating an e-mail policy: when to send messages, when not to; what's the expected turnaround time for an e-mail; how lengthy an e-mail should be before it becomes onerous to read, and so forth.

9 Make judicious use of the human moment, that is, face-to-face communication. While more expensive and cumbersome, human moments are infinitely richer and more powerful than electronic moments.

10 Measure and monitor your progress. The more progress you make, the more motivated you'll feel to continue to cut back on screen sucking. Monitor not only the time you save, but also the increase in the volume and quality of your work that you will most assuredly enjoy.

2

multitasking

how to say no when you have
more to do than time to do it

Jean hit the snooze button again. How many more times could she hit it before she had to get up? Each time she pushed the button she got ten more blessed minutes of sleep before being reawakened by a hissing blast of radio static. She'd been so tired the night before that she'd pushed a wrong button on their new system. She didn't yet know how to tune it properly to her favorite station, and she hadn't wanted to interrupt her husband's TV show to ask him to do it for her.

"You're a big girl, you can figure it out," Lou would have responded, implying that she was both technologically incompetent and, worse, lazy. So she'd gone to sleep knowing she'd be awakened this cold winter morning by static. So deep was her desire for sleep—those treasured, tender, loving arms of sleep—that she hadn't cared.

Now the question she faced was how many more ten-minute blocks of snooze-button sleep she could wangle from her conscience before the combination of guilt and necessity "drug her out" of bed, as her Kentucky-bred father would have said. Two snoozes later, she was in the shower, while Lou, who'd slept through the static, began to stir. Standing with her eyes closed, facing up into the bracing blast of water coming from the shower head—she and Lou shared a love of a strong shower— she wished the shower could last all day. Here was one place she could be alone and uninterrupted. Alone with her thoughts, she often did her best thinking and planning here.

When she finally turned off the water and stepped out, Lou slapped her affectionately on her butt and said, "Long shower, hon. You leave me any hot water?"

"Sorry," Jean said. "I got lost in my thoughts."

Fifteen minutes later, she'd somehow done her hair and makeup. She frowned disapprovingly at her bloated face in the mirror, knowing that she really, really needed to shed a good twenty pounds. "I've *got* to get to the gym again," she thought, as she hastily slipped on her underwear, skirt, blouse, jacket, and shoes.

She rushed downstairs to the kitchen to prepare breakfast for Lily and Isabel while Lou got ready to go to the hospital. She and Lou had a routine that worked, even though it seemed to Jean that it worked better for Lou than for her. Even so, she loved him and her girls. She just wasn't sure how much she loved her life.

———————

Part of Jean's responsibility was also to make sure her daughters actually did get downstairs. Now in the third and fifth grades, respectively, they each had chores. Lily's job was to make sure Bouncy, their calico cat, got her tin of wet food, while Isabel fed Falstaff, their black Lab. It would have been easier for Jean to feed the pets herself, but she was trying to teach her girls to be responsible. They already took it for granted that their breakfast would be waiting for them when they arrived downstairs.

People who fit the category of ADT outlined in this chapter tend to agree with the following statements.

I can't get my work done without multitasking.

Saying no is very hard for me to do.

I'd own my own company or be in charge of the one I work at now if I could just manage my time more effectively.

If I could just get organized, I'd be far more successful.

If only I could clone myself, I'd be fine.

At work, I have more trouble than the average person in preventing interruptions.

I wish people at work would leave me alone so I could get stuff done.

Oh, what I'd give for just one uninterrupted hour.

"Maybe you could give them the responsibility of making their own breakfasts?" Lou had suggested in exasperation. But since no one had made Jean breakfast when she was growing up, she was determined to make sure that Lily and Isabel got a nourishing breakfast every day. It gave her a special satisfaction to do more for her kids than her parents had done for her.

Upon hitting the kitchen every morning, the first thing Jean did was unplug her smartphone from its charger and check her e-mail. She'd become so adept manipulating her phone that it became like an appendage. She could scramble eggs with one hand and operate the phone with the other, thus getting a jump on the day's messages while still providing her kids with a hot meal.

As usual, a problem popped up in the first e-mail. "Jean, will need you immediately. Terrence is in a swoon. Let me know the second you get here. Thanks. Mort."

A graduate of Harvard Law School, Jean had taken a nonpartner track position at a Boston firm so she could take care of the girls and accommodate Lou's lifelong ambition to pursue a career in academic medicine like his father. Life at a teaching hospital, especially for doctors on the way up, could be mentally brutal and physically exhausting, so Lou didn't have as much time with his family as he'd like. Jean was glad to make up the difference. At least, she told herself and the rest of the world she was.

Her flexible job meant that she was on call for the partners all day. Her informal job description at the firm was "crisis manager and trouble shooter" for whichever partner nabbed her first. She was so good at thinking on her feet, so smart, and so adept at dealing with difficult people that she'd become the go-to person for all manner of thorny problems, often unrelated to law, the partners wanted help with. Much of her time was spent in a gray zone that didn't fall under the billable hours of legal service. This meant that she was both overworked and underpaid.

She contemplated how many hours of hand-holding and ego-boosting Terrence, a hugely gifted but massively needy client, this current problem would require. She resented Mort for making Terrence's problems her problems. "I've *got* to speak to Jim about this," she muttered to herself, tapping her foot in annoyance.

As the girls inhaled their eggs, she put on her coat and went to the garage to warm up the car, as the thermometer had dipped below twenty degrees. The girls went to two different schools, so Jean had to make two separate stops, not close to each other, before she parked her car and took the subway downtown.

Once on the Red Line, she had a good thirty minutes to herself. She might have lost herself in a novel, but instead she chose to complete reading her backlog of e-mails and send out replies to them and the early-bird texts. Though she was already working, she still treasured the thirty-minute ride as her own time. It gave her the illusion that she was running her own show.

"Imagine that," she said to herself. "I look forward to riding the subway. *What's my life become?*"

As she got off the train, she heard her phone ring. She didn't recognize the ring tone or the number. "Better answer," she thought, worrying that one of her girls might be in trouble.

"Hello, Jean!" It was the development officer from Isabel's school who, following some lovely, flattering talk about what a great kid Isabel was, proceeded to ask Jean if she'd consider chairing the annual auction again. Flustered, Jean couldn't think of an excuse fast enough before saying that she was honored that the school thought of her for the job, that of course she'd run the auction, and that it was the least she could do, considering how good the school had been for Isabel.

After she clicked "END," she felt like crying. But she allowed no tears. No *time* for tears. Instead, she breezed through the revolving doors of One International Place, bought her usual no-fat latte at her usual spot—she loved that moment of casual connection with Ashley, the barista—and rode the elevator to the thirty-eighth floor. "How I love this ride," she mused to herself as the elevator whooshed its way skyward. "If only the office were on the *one thousand thirty-eighth* floor!"

life in a prison of ADT

Jean's life is typical of that of millions of people who feel they must sacrifice themselves every day to the small stuff at the expense of their own needs. In the process, they risk their health, their relationships, and their jobs. Why does this happen?

life in hyper-speed

Let's take a closer look at the ways Jean's ADT specifically worked against her. Overcommitted, overworked, chronically stressed and tired, but with no chance to slow down, she could no longer call her life her own. Rather, her life comprised a bundle of responses to other people's requests and demands that would assail her in an endless torrent.

She was wasting her great mind. Blessed with an IQ that had been tested in school as 149, she was "way smart," as her brother would say. When Lou married her, she was slim, beautiful, fun, ambitious, and lively. She received shining reviews at work. But she was also conscientiously hyper-responsive, making herself the potential victim of her own good intentions, her own noble ambitions, her own interests and loves. Her hyper-responsiveness meant that her attention flitted from topic to topic, interruption to interruption, distraction to distraction, staying put only seconds at a time. She was so used to being interrupted that she grew unable to pay attention to anything or anyone for very long. She often jumped the gun and looked elsewhere before the distraction had even arrived, not because she had attention deficit disorder, but because she had "conscientious-surplus disorder." *She didn't want to miss a thing*, any possible chance to please, serve, or be of value.

Like so many suffering from ADT, Jean couldn't pay attention because the mental muscles that attention requires had weakened or atrophied. Her attention vectored here and there, as if pulled by hundreds of invisible magnets. When her husband, children, or boss asked her for her full attention, she could no more give it than she could sit down and write a letter by hand. She once knew how to do it, but to try to do it now would only cause frustration.

Jean couldn't even get out of bed on her own terms, but had to bargain with herself for a few minutes more of sleep. She accommodated her husband, her children, the partners at her office, and the development officer at her daughter's school all before she even arrived at her workplace.

In addition to feeling that she was responsible *for* everything, Jean also felt that she had to respond *to* everything, right here and right now. This led to even more dangerous problems. For example, Jean's tendency to have so many projects going simultaneously—at work, with her children, in the community, with her spouse—meant that it was impossible for her to do her best on any of them. Because the default position in ADT is "fast," Jean was also reflexively impatient. Waiting for anything caused her pain. Fast felt right. Slow hurt.

The culture of modern life reinforced all this in Jean. She took odd pride in being hurried, having more to do than time to do it, being so in demand. Because she felt guilty relaxing, she busied herself at every turn—cleaning the kitchen, tidying up the closets, brushing the dog—even when there was no pressing need to do any of these things.

Living her life at hyper-speed impaired her sense of time. She always *felt* she was in a hurry, no matter what the clock said. On the other hand, her desire to get as much done in as short a time as possible was so intense that she often imagined she could do more in, say, five minutes than any human possibly could, leading her often to fall short and feel like a failure.

For Jean and for the many others like her, lingering over anything became all but impossible. Jean had to juggle so much that she had trouble clearing the mental space even to listen to others. She completed others' sentences; she interrupted them. (This was no surprise, because her life was one long interruption; in her worldview, that was "reality.") She was so eager to complete whatever conversation she was having in order to get on to the next obligation that she hurried the dialogue along however she could.

If the conversation—or the traffic, or the line at the grocery store—moved too slowly, she felt she would explode. More than once, she'd left a supermarket, her shopping cart still full, because she couldn't bear how slow the line was. And more than once, she'd suddenly demanded someone to get to the point, losing her alliance with that person in the process.

Over time, the stress began to take its inevitable toll. Whenever Jean felt tired or blocked in her race to keep up, she felt that she had to put more pedal to the metal. Working harder supplanted working smarter, as it always does with strung-out people. She stopped going to the gym because she felt she didn't have time for even twenty minutes of daily exercise. For her, working harder and staying up later became what she considered her only viable solution, spinning her into an even more desperate frenzy.

Recognizing that things were going wrong, Jean stole some time to peruse a few self-help books in search of a solution. She didn't have time to see a therapist; the closest she got was Joey, her hairdresser and most cherished guilty pleasure. She looked at books on time management, organization, parenting, self-assertion, and anything else that seemed even remotely relevant to her predicament, but none of the books hit the mark. They seemed intended for a simple-minded audience that Jean could not relate to.

She actually believed she could manage time just fine. She could organize her stuff, the kids' stuff, and Lou's stuff, but there was not enough time in the day to keep up with everything. Despite the fact that someone came twice a month to clean the house, she felt as if she were always cleaning up other people's messes.

She thought she knew how to be a good parent, and she *was* a good parent, even though she felt guilty she didn't do more. She knew she was not exercising enough, that she was eating too much and not taking good care of herself, but she believed all she had to do was change those habits. She didn't need a book to tell her that. Furthermore, most of the books stressed being assertive, but she could assert herself just fine. And to whom, exactly, was she supposed to assert herself to fix up her life? God?

Come bedtime, all she wanted to do was sleep. Lou was no longer the loving, sexy husband whose bones she once wanted to jump. She used to love to lie in his arms and bury her head into his chest. Now he was just that body lying on the other side of the mattress. ADT had poisoned her relationship with her spouse.

Jean enters the DANGER zone

"I guess you forgot I turned a year older today," Lou said very quietly one night as they were getting into bed.

Jean had completely forgotten his birthday.

Instead of apologizing, she snapped. "I can't remember *everything*, you know, and aren't you a little *old* to be worrying about a *birthday?* Should I have baked a cake and invited all your friends and put little hats on all of you so you could blow out all your candles and sing 'Happy Birthday'? Why don't you help me out instead of worrying about your damn birthday? Do you know how much I sacrifice so you can pursue your precious academic career? Do you know how much crap I have to put up with so you can follow in your perfect father's footsteps? Do you have any idea how much stress I carry around so you can worry about your fucking *birthday?*"

Had Jean been in her right mind following her tirade, she would have realized what she had done and apologized for taking out on Lou the frustrations that had built up in her all day, all week, all year. But she did not apologize, and Lou said nothing. He simply got out of bed and went to sleep in the guest bedroom.

The marriage would survive, but it would ache for a long time.

As her to-do lists grew longer, and Lou, feeling hurt, withdrew support, she slept less and worried more. The worrying became an ambient noise; she went to sleep with it and woke up with it. Her stressful feelings hung like a cowl over her head, darkening the atmosphere in the house.

The more she had to do, the more she procrastinated, and the more her productivity suffered. Her boss noticed, and said so in her performance review.

Depressed, Jean began to spin out of control. Her lack of exercise soon led her to feel less alert and more in need of some other kind of "fix," so she turned to the comforts of macaroni and cheese, pizza, and fried chicken. She didn't give a damn. "Let me be fat. *Really* fat! Why not?" she thought. "Who cares?" She didn't dare get on the scales. Her weight gain made her even crankier, so she started to drink three or four glasses of wine each evening. The alcohol impaired the quality of the little sleep she did manage to get, so she awoke more tired and with a hangover. She was in greater danger than she knew.

Since Lou had begun spending more long nights at the hospital, Jean started to flirt with random people: the checkout guy at Whole Foods, the gas station attendant who always eyed her and whose butt she liked, and the older gentleman at the liquor store who so reminded her of her high school English teacher. She didn't go so far as to have an affair, but she realized that she was giving off signals she couldn't control.

She began to feel physically ill as well. She developed aches and pains in her neck and lower back, pains she'd never had before, and had indigestion after every meal, as well as often between meals. Her sense of zest and vitality, long her trademarks, all but disappeared.

Now and then a colleague or a friend would ask her gently if anything was wrong. "Why do you ask?" she'd snap, defensively. "So I've put on a few pounds. So I'm not a slave to the ridiculous image the media makes women aspire to. Fact is, I'm proud to be me." The inquiring person would learn not to inquire again. Increasingly, Jean became isolated and alone.

Jean entered what I call the DANGER zone, an acronym summarized as:

D—disappointment, defeat leads to . . .

A—anger and blame leads to . . .

N—negativity leads to . . .

G—globalizing of negative feelings leads to . . .

E—escape into wasteful or dangerous activities leads to . . .

R—rejection of help, of others, of life

In the DANGER zone, everything in a person's life comes under threat. So it was with Jean. Her marriage, her kids' well-being, her job, and even her life itself all hung in the balance.

the children of ADT: Jean's backstory

Usually, the worldview that children develop when they are young persists throughout their lives. But what we do as children to help us cope with life at home can become maladaptive in adulthood. As with the other characters in this book, this was the case with Jean.

Jean was the fourth of six siblings. She grew up in an era when parents didn't pay much attention to kids, certainly not doting on them as they do now. She recalled her grandmother sternly admonishing her when she asked for a story during the adults' sacrosanct cocktail hour. "Jean, you must learn that children should be seen and not heard. Run along now and let the grownups talk."

Her parents were good people, but they were busy themselves and didn't fuss over her. She never had to worry about what grades she got in school, because her parents barely noticed and because school was easy anyway. She didn't have to worry about passing inspection on her clothes because she dressed herself from an early age, made her own breakfast, and headed out the door to the school bus, often without even a goodbye, let alone a kiss.

She didn't feel neglected; this was just the way life was. Looking back, she realized she had faced a choice as a child. Like so many of our most important choices, it was not a conscious choice, but it was undeniably a choice. She could get the attention she so craved from her parents in one of two ways. She could be *bad*, or she could be *good*. Her two older brothers chose bad; stealing and getting into trouble with drugs gained them a lot of attention. But Jean hadn't wanted that kind of attention. So she chose *good*.

Being good gradually took her over and became part of her wiring, her psychic DNA, so that being anything but good became all but impossible. Jean also learned that saying yes and being accommodating was taken to be a sign of good character and virtue. From her Girl Scout leaders and schoolteachers, she learned that it was important to contribute above and beyond. Such beliefs ruled her in her adult life; if she failed to meet others' expectations, not to mention her own, impossible though they may have been, she blamed herself and felt guilty for what she hadn't done. Her self-esteem then took a hit. And if she ever had time to slow down and goof off, she didn't take it for fear of violating her code, as if committing a serious sin.

The entrenched need to say yes and to be good meant that, for her, saying no felt as foreign and impossible as waking up speaking Swahili or feeling that she had turned into a bird. She really couldn't comprehend not fulfilling everyone's requests of her. It was painful to even imagine telling her boss that she might be unreachable during the weekend, or telling her kids that she couldn't be interrupted when she was in the shower.

Ironically, by the time Jean was in the DANGER zone, this "good girl" who had said yes to everything and everyone—and who had so sought approval—was no longer approved of. She was coming apart.

TABLE 2-1

Beneficial and problematic characteristics of multitaskers and people who can't say no

Beneficial	Problematic
Attentive to all that's going on, you don't want to miss anything	Too attentive to everything, you are unable to pay full attention to anything
Responsible, conscientious	Hyper-responsible; you feel responsible even when you're not
Ambitious, a desire to get a lot done	Tendency to take on more than you can reasonably handle
Active, a desire to jump in and get involved	Too active; you jump in too many directions
A desire to stay on top of news, issues, fashions	A preoccupation with the latest thing, what the Joneses are doing, what's au courant
Caring, empathic, tuned in to the feelings of others	Too empathic, too tuned in, so you are unable to give enough attention to self and the primary others in your life
A desire to work hard and make a contribution	A feeling of never having done enough, an inability to feel fulfilled and content
A love of life	An inability to linger over life's beautiful moments

what is beneficial? what isn't?

Useful qualities can become problematic in most people who allow modern life to spin them into ADT. Jean's backstory—her childhood—created susceptibility to ADT, but then the conditions of modern life created the full-blown condition. Table 2-1 shows how beneficial, adaptive behavior can become problematic in the case of ADT.

The good news is that people with ADT have a lot of grit and resilience. They usually find a way out of the DANGER zone. Of course, I am talking about the people who self-select to consult with me, the resourceful ones who can admit that they have a problem and are willing to seek help. By the time they see me, it's almost certain that the worst is over and they are already on their way back to a more peaceful state of mind. The ones who do collapse and lose most of what they have are the people who refuse to seek help and allow themselves to become so isolated that they implode.

In Jean's case, she became unable to follow the basic plan because her energy was so low that none of the other elements were possible. Her challenge was simply in freeing up time to sleep, eat, exercise, and preserve some downtime, perhaps even make love.

The challenge was, as it is with everyone struggling to regain focus, both psychological and strategic. I had to encourage her to give herself permission not to please everyone all the time. I concentrated both on helping her learn new structures that would save her time and on helping her learn how to allow herself to say no rather than to always say yes.

One example of the new structures I taught her is the acronym CDE, which stands for "curtail, delegate, eliminate." I also encouraged her to speak directly to her supervisor; she needed to change her job description so that she was not at everyone's beck and call. But to do this, she had to short-circuit her yes-responder. How I help a person do this varies, but I usually combine encouragement with role-playing, followed by the person testing the new behavior out in real life and then reporting back what worked well.

The reason Jean hadn't tried any of this before was because on the deepest level, she feared that saying no risked her losing everything. Saying no, to her, represented a forbidden breach of the rules she'd followed her entire life.

As I said earlier, much of our adult behavior is rooted in what we had to do as children, imagined we had to do, were told we had to do, or all of the above, in order to get what we needed to survive. Jean now had to learn that the rules of her childhood no longer applied, that now, in fact, it was safe to say no. Indeed, it was a really good idea to say no. But it took a crisis, her near unraveling, before she felt the desperation of being shipwrecked. Although she did not hit bottom, she came close enough to break down her ingrained style of coping. In pain, she reached for a new idea, for something to which to cling. It was simply this: *I want a life for myself.* She became like the character in the movie *Network* who screamed out his window, "I'm mad as hell and I'm not gonna take it anymore." That anger would set her free. But it took a lot of heat to melt the door of the vault she'd put that anger into.

In terms of the basic plan, Jean's issues created the following problems:

1. ENERGY. Jean was run ragged by her insistence on being the perfect good girl, the one who got everything done and done well.

2. EMOTION. Anger built up in her as inevitably as debt builds up when you overspend.

3. ENGAGEMENT. She overengaged. She couldn't focus long enough on anything to tend to it well.

4. STRUCTURE. Jean's emotional makeup prevented her from setting up the structures and boundaries that could save her.

5. CONTROL. She gave over control to her fastidious sense of duty and her compulsion to please others.

WHAT TO DO ABOUT IT

10 tips for multitaskers and people who can't say no

---

① It is neurologically impossible to concentrate on two tasks at once. What people really mean by "multitasking" is switching attention from one task to another in rapid succession. If both tasks are boring, like talking to a dull person on your cellphone while unloading the dishwasher, then you can get away with it. But if either or both of the tasks are complex, like talking to a smart person on your cellphone while writing a report on a complicated investment, then both the conversation and the report will suffer, as will you.

2   It's fun to multitask, and it gives the illusion of saving time, which is why so many people talk on their phones while doing e-mail and also following the stream on their Bloomberg Terminals. But beware; you may feel like a master of the universe while you do it, but the chances that you will miss critical information rise exponentially with each task you add.

3   On the other hand, you can multitask when what you're doing is either autonomically mediated, like breathing and maintaining balance in a chair, or requires no concentration, like taking a shower while listening to music on an iPod. Indeed, strictly speaking, we all multitask, even when we're asleep, as our minds and bodies are always doing many things.

4   Multitasking is only dangerous when one or more of the tasks requires attention and focus in the present moment—and then it's as dangerous as drinking and driving. For example, you can drive your car while listening to your radio, but you better take your focus off the radio when you get close to your exit or you're likely to drive past it, unless you know the route on automatic pilot. But texting while in a meeting or, worse, while driving, may cost you dearly.

5   The inability to say no, which is an occupational hazard of kind and conscientious people, can put you into a perpetual state of overload. Practice politely declining requests.

6 A good way to say no is to say, "I'd love to do that if I had the time, but as it is, I could not give it the attention it deserves, so I would not be able to perform as well as you and the task warrant."

7 Explain to yourself that it is right, good, and proper to say no. If you always say yes, you will soon burn out and be of little use to your organization, your family, or yourself.

8 Learn to delegate. The goal in today's world is not to be independent but to be interdependent in such a way that you give as much as you get.

9 Element three in the basic plan, engagement, happens most easily when you are doing what you are good at and what you like to do. Say yes to those opportunities.

10 Understand that you do everyone a favor when you say no. You are simply stating that you are not the person who is best for that task at the present time. The organization benefits by knowing that and should thank you.

idea hopping

how to finish what you start

"No, no, no, no, no!" Brian yelled. "I can't go down this road again. I've told you I'll back you in whatever you want to do, but I can't back you anymore in refusing to make up your mind."

"Brian, I'm not refusing. I just *can't*. Please understand."

"I can't understand! Believe me, I've tried. Right now it's pretty hard for me not to see you just as a spoiled, rich woman who's nothing but a dilettante."

Ashley felt stunned, as if hit with a brick. "Screw you, Brian. What a horrible thing for you to say. Life's no problem for you because things come easily to you. You might offer me some understanding instead of your smug little judgments."

"Ashley, I'm sorry. You're right. What I said was mean. But I'm just so frustrated, I don't know what to say."

"*You're* frustrated? How do you think *I* feel? It's *my* life I'm wasting."

"Well, not your whole life. The kids and me count for something, I hope."

"Of course you do. But how would you feel if you had no career, even though you had instant access to all the backing you could ever need, but all you could come up with was ideas with no follow-through? I feel like a two-year-old. I can't stick with anything."

Ashley and Brian had a strict rule never to go to bed angry, so when they shut off the light at 11:00, he reached out to her and she snuggled into the crook of his shoulder. He stroked her back gently. "I love you," he said, giving her a soft kiss. Then he turned on his side. Soon, his breathing slowed, and he was fast asleep.

As usual, Ashley lay wide awake, staring at the ceiling, listening to the sound of the crickets outside. She could feel tears in the corners of her eyes. She knew Brian was right. She was a rich man's spoiled wife. And she was a dilettante. She'd never had the stick-to-itiveness, or whatever it took, to follow through on a project. It wasn't that her ideas weren't good; it was just that she had too many of them and, like a bee in a garden full of flowers, as soon as she landed on a sweet-smelling red rose of a concept, she was distracted by the tall blue delphinium of another cool idea, or the honeysuckle lining the fence with more ideas.

Why couldn't she stick with one flower long enough to follow through?

She most definitely had the entrepreneurial itch, which is almost always associated with symptoms of ADT. But her version of ADT brought to mind the nursery rhyme about the old woman who lived in a shoe, only in this instance, she had so many *ideas* she didn't know what to do. Ideas swirled in Ashley's head like a pile of dead leaves hit by a gust of wind. As soon as she tried capturing and arranging them, another gust would scatter them.

People who fit the category of ADT outlined in this chapter tend to agree with the following statements.

I have so many ideas, I don't know what to do with them all.

I love the start of projects and the conclusion. It's the middle I have trouble with.

I stay awake at night with new ideas running through my mind.

I avoid doing difficult work by doing busywork.

My actions can't keep up with my imagination.

I get bored when the novelty of a new project wears off.

My biggest problem is learning how to prioritize.

My problem is that nothing grabs me enough for me to stick with it when it gets boring.

Ashley's idea factory

Ashley met and married Brian, the founder of a successful Silicon Valley start-up, while she was in graduate school. When she was pregnant with their first child, she started selling stuff on eBay and did pretty well at it. But she didn't stick with that. Then, after the birth of her son, she teamed up with another woman to start an online travel business catering to young families, but she was never able to get traction with that. Then she wanted to work with an animator to develop a graphic design software business, but the business plan floundered.

She was actually good at writing business plans. She could knock them out in short order. In the past year, she'd researched and written two solid plans for new businesses. One was based on office furniture. She had an idea for a conventional office desk that, with the flick of a switch, could be converted into a standing desk, or even into a treadmill desk. Given the increasing amount of research showing the benefits of standing while working or walking very slowly, she knew the idea would take off. She also came up with an idea for a compact, pullout bed that could be tucked under a desk, perfect for night owls and late-working techies.

Then there was the lingerie, which she invented while making love one night with Brian: the silk stockings that stayed firmly in place and didn't slide down to the top of a woman's knees and the gossamer-light silk-and-mohair robe, perfect for chilly nights in front of the fire.

Ashley had fallen in love with each of these ideas, as well as dozens more that flitted through her mind. Her brain hummed like a round-the-clock dream factory. She often lay awake at night—not worrying, but in a constant state of excitement that felt almost sexual, like going to meet someone on a first date. She wanted to get up and write a proposal, but before she could do that, another idea flew up out of the pile of leaves, and she had to follow that one. "Do you know what it's like?" she told a friend. "It's a major turn-on; it's really fun to make these ideas grow in my mind, especially because I know every one of them could turn into a successful business, maybe a home run. What's killing me is the trouble I have in turning any idea into reality!"

Ashley's inability to follow through was certainly not due to a lack of resources. She was a dynamic, smart woman who was also a mother of two school-age children and supervisor to a live-in nanny. Her husband was the son of the founder of a mammoth insurance company, so there was plenty of family money that got spread around, and her husband had made good money himself.

Ashley developed her business plans because she wanted to, not because she had to. With an MBA from Stanford, she delighted in conceiving little businesses out of a passion that dated back to childhood. Now, after years of following her dreams but never catching them, Ashley found that her energy and creativity could carry her only so far. She found it almost impossible to pick a favorite idea and then focus on developing just that one. Worse, she seemed to become more and more sidetracked the older she got, which led to increasing difficulty sweating the details. She also had trouble delegating. While she was briefly focused on one thing, she dove in with everything she had; but having done that, she felt lost, hoping that others would jump in and magically finish the project for her.

She understood Brian's frustration; after all, he'd been through his own tough times to make his dreams come true. But he had succeeded. Now he was a multimillionaire of his own making. She was frustrated that she couldn't make it as well. She yearned to be like Debbi Fields with her cookies, or Anita Roddick with The Body Shop, or Tory Burch with her amazing line from shoes to sunglasses, or Sara Blakely, the world's youngest female self-made billionaire with her Spanx. But the journey from dream to reality was unbearably long and, Ashley had to admit, much too tedious for her. She understood the pain of doctoral candidates who had long dissertations to finish in which they had utterly lost interest, or of wannabe novelists who could not write past chapter three.

the despair of infinite possibility

The late Leston Havens, longtime professor of psychiatry at Harvard and one of the best teachers I ever had, once said to me, "You can do a whole psychotherapy centered around one question. 'What do you want?' Choosing which of those four words to put emphasis on— 'what,' 'do,' 'you,' or 'want'—takes the discussion in four completely different directions."

In Ashley's case, the question that tormented her most would put the emphasis on the second word, "do." "Ashley, what *do* you want?" She'd asked herself that question at least a thousand times.

Answering Havens' deceptively simple question can take anywhere from a moment to a lifetime. Some people never answer it, which can feel much worse than answering it but never getting what you want. If you can't answer it at all, you are left to wander forever with no destination in mind.

In his book *The Sickness Unto Death*, the existential Christian philosopher Søren Kierkegaard described what he called "the despair of infinite possibility."[1] If the theme of life's possibilities should bring a person to despair, it is usually because the possibilities in that person's life are finite, leaving the person always wanting more. Alexander the Great famously despaired, for example, when he could see no more worlds to conquer.

However, some people despair not because their possibilities are limited, but rather because they are infinite. While taking care of life's necessities binds most of us to one task after another, some people do not allow necessity to put the brakes on their imaginations. They continue to imagine one possibility after another, even though none of them becomes reality. As Kierkegaard put it, "more and more becomes possible because *nothing becomes actual*" [emphasis mine].

While the labor required to grow one idea into actuality engages most people and keeps them from turning to another project for a while, the person caught in infinite possibility despairs because she beholds nothing but opportunities. For her, the usually optimistic phrase "anything's possible" tolls like a death knell.

What keeps "infinite possibility" people from turning the possible into the actual is not just that they are well off and don't have to make money or they don't have to please a boss; those are usually just the surface reasons. One deeper reason is that they may lack the skills, the cognitive apparatus to get things done. Kathy Kolbe's research on "conation" has proven that people differ on a genetic basis in their inborn styles of attacking problems.[2] Conation is the most powerful idea in psychology that no one's ever heard of. Each person has his or her own "conative style." Your conative style is your inborn style of addressing a project or solving a problem. We've all heard of cognition (thinking) and affect (feeling), but few people have heard of the third element in the trio, conation, your natural style of getting something done.

A simple way to determine your own conative style is to perform the following thought experiment. Imagine a person dumps a wheelbarrow full of junk on the floor in front of you. Now you have before you a pile of random odds and ends, bits of scrap metal, pieces of cloth, some loose buttons, a light bulb, some small wheels, orange peels, dog bones, a bicycle chain, a felt Fedora, an old can of 3-IN-ONE oil, a piece of driftwood, a lobster claw minus the meat, some egg shells, a tattered paperback copy of *Huckleberry Finn*, a treadless tire, an empty picture frame, an air horn, and a pair of ancient wooden snow shoes with leather lacings. "Make something out of this pile of junk," the person then says to you.

What you do next is determined by your conative style. One person will ask, "Why should I?" Another will ask, "What is this object you want me to make meant to do?" Another will inquire as to the person's motivation in requesting the junk be assembled into something. Another person will immediately start to sort the junk into various categories. Yet another will simply tidy it up and remove any debris. Someone else will ask for help and ask if it's OK to make a phone call or to use reference material. Someone else will stand in stony silence, pondering the pile, while another will walk around it taking it in from different angles. Someone else might photograph it with his iPhone and send it along to his engineer buddy, while yet another person will simply burst out laughing. Another will start drawing up a plan on the palm of his hand. And there are always some people who immediately dive in and start assembling parts with no conscious design in mind whatsoever (those are usually entrepreneurs, by the way).

There is no right response to the request. But the great variety in possible responses points up how widely people can vary one from another in the realm of conation. If you think of all that goes into taking an idea from its inception to its completion, it is no wonder that few people indeed can do it all alone, just by themselves, as few people have the cognitive, conative, or affective range to do everything involved in taking a project from initial idea to completed product solo.

Ashley's conative style does not include the ability to get things done on her own. That's not a moral failing, rather a feature of her inborn conative style. Rather than trying to be someone she is not, she needs to get the right helpers or partners. Instead, she gets sidetracked and lands in despair. Rather than rejoicing in her mind's fertility, she finally fears that all she will ever do is give birth to stillborn ideas. As the poet John Greenleaf Whittier wrote, "For all the sad words of tongue or pen, / The saddest are these: 'It might have been.'"

The despair of infinite possibility, in its half-lit gloom, is the despair of knowing what might have been but never came to be. What sharpens the despair is the individual blaming himself. Far from not taking responsibility, he takes too much responsibility, excoriating himself for his inability to reach his goals.

Ashley's torment is, in fact, rooted in her great strength, her imagination. Her "hunger of the imagination," to use Samuel Johnson's fervent phrase, could never be sated, even as it gorged itself endlessly upon her life. What most people would consider a gift grew into a curse for Ashley.

Like most born entrepreneurs, Ashley had great talent and energy. She embodied the best of what makes a free enterprise system work. She loved opportunity, embraced self-reliance, gladly took on risk, loved to work hard, treasured a huge reward, and felt entitled to nothing but the honest fruits of her own labor. Until things begin to fall apart for her, she wasn't dissuaded by failure. Like a fisherman who comes back empty-handed, she simply got up early the next morning to try again.

But she failed to answer the important questions that could help her even more than the latest-model fish finder. "*Why* am I bringing home fewer fish than I want? And *where* can I look for help?"

Ashley's backstory

Ashley's form of ADT, the despair of infinite possibility, is especially common today because, due to electronic communication technology, so much more has become possible than ever before. The great blessing of modern life can also be its curse: you can do so much. The possibilities line up in an endlessly sparkling, flashing, pinging array, perpetually distracting a person like Ashley, creating a particularly modern kind of ADT.

As usual, more than just modern life caused her form of ADT. As a child, Ashley was intelligent and curious. Though slightly overweight, she was nonetheless immediately engaging and attractive. Her inner energy made her eyes sparkle, and most people were instantly attracted by her creativity liveliness. She was often the life of the party, witty, funny, and enthusiastic. She had been a risk taker since high school and college, when she'd happily take a dare to bungee jump off a fifty-foot bridge or go parasailing.

Ashley was an entrepreneur long before she even knew what the word meant. She did it naturally, without encouragement, the way some prodigies pick up a violin and start to play it. One summer day at the age of ten, she put up the best summer lemonade stand anyone in her WASPy, upper-middle-class Connecticut neighborhood had ever seen. She took her lemonade stand to a whole new level by making it look like a real patio. Her brothers helped her drag out lawn chairs and a large plastic table from the garage. They shaded it with a big beach umbrella. Ashley added a fan, homemade chocolate-chip cookies, and a bowl of nuts, all paid for from her allowance. She filled up a wading pool that customers could dip their toes in, brought out a CD-playing boom box that filled the air with the Beach Boys, the Beatles, and, for jazz lovers, John Coltrane. Ashley's customers, walking or biking by, appreciated the chance to sit down in the shade and listen to music while sipping their cold drink.

Upon coming home from her social club and finding the scene on her front lawn, Ashley's mother, a Protestant of Mayflower lineage, and the parent in charge, was horrified. Embarrassed by Ashley's front-lawn "spectacle," she forced Ashley to take it all down. Later that evening, finding Ashley in tears, her father, Preston, argued with his wife. "For Pete's sake, Daphne," Preston urged, "the kid is creative. The neighbors love it. Just let her have some fun. It's summer."

Daphne, of course, prevailed. She always did.

Preston was a top-notch orthopedic surgeon. Ashley adored her father but, since he was a busy doctor, he was unable to pay much attention to her. When he came home, he tended to retreat into his office, where he would listen to Willy Nelson albums with his headset on. Still, Ashley took strength from him, even though she saw little of him.

Preston's prestigious, high-paying job allowed Daphne to be invited to elite social clubs. An aspiring socialite, Daphne favored Ashley's older brothers, who fit the image of top-drawer males to a T. Blond, trim, and naturally confident, the boys did well in their studies and in sports. They were "perfect," as Daphne would often say. Daphne thanked the God she pretended to worship at the local Congregational church every Sunday for her boys, who performed like proper keys to the kingdom she actually did worship, the kingdom of Connecticut's, and by extension the world's, social elite.

To her mother, Ashley was embarrassingly imperfect: Daphne openly criticized Ashley for being too undisciplined, too chubby, too distracted, too silly, and not nearly beautiful or polished enough to take her place in high society. While Ashley's brothers achieved at a consistently high level, Ashley's grades shot up and down. Ashley attended the same private school as her brothers, but she did not achieve their superior academic performance. Her counselors and teachers told her that she could get top grades all the time if she applied herself a bit more.

Though she was marvelously creative, Ashley was not the kind of kid who could buckle down and study boring assignments or drive single-mindedly toward one goal. When people asked her what she wanted to do when she grew up, she always had fifty-five different answers; later on, when they asked her what her major in college would be, she just rolled her eyes.

In Daphne's eyes, Ashley was a clumsy, chubby tomboy, and a little on the dim side. "You know as well as I do what a disappointment you are to me," she once actually told Ashley. "But you can be sure I will not allow you to hold this family back from the place in this world we deserve. I won't let it happen." At that, Daphne snapped her fingers, as if summoning a servant to remove a mess, turned on her heel, and strode away.

Ashley collapsed into a heap of tears. But thereafter, when her mother would insult her in similarly cruel ways, she narrowed her eyes and determinedly recited to herself what her first-grade teacher had taught the class: "I am the boss of myself. I will not let mean words hurt me." It worked.

Ashley's resilience

Against major odds, Ashley was able to fight off her competitive mother's negativity, for several reasons.

First, she was lucky enough to be born with genes that predisposed her to optimism, spunk, grit, the capacity to generate ideas, and an entrepreneurial drive. We know now that all of these qualities, while not entirely determined by genes, get a running start at birth if a person is born with the right combination of nucleic acids. Though Ashley secretly hated her nickname—"Spunky"—because she thought it implied that she was highly energetic but not so bright, her spunky resiliency and imagination helped her to carry on.

Second, she had a loving connection with her father. The power of just a single positive connection, of the kind Ashley had with Preston, can diminish and even cancel out the damage done by a negative connection.

While Preston was not deeply involved in her upbringing, he was there, and just being there counts for a lot. She interacted with him just enough so that she took strength, day after day, year after year, simply from his being her father and her being his only daughter. Even when he was not around, Ashley's adoration worked its way through her system all the time with the coursing of her blood, like the invaluable growth-force connection truly is.

Under the right conditions, this kind of adoration can save the soul. A person can draw life-saving sustenance by adoring someone—even if the beloved doesn't interact much with the one doing the adoring—as long as the connection is beneficent and reciprocally acknowledged.

Third, Ashley was lucky enough to go a school that valued thinking over memorization and playing with ideas over listening to a teacher talk. Ashley learned to love to think and experiment. Even though her grades were too mediocre to put her on the honor roll, she delighted in school and did well enough to get accepted to Stanford. She decided to major in economics, stayed on to get her MBA, and took to business school like fingers to a piano. At B-school, she found the instrument she wanted to play the rest of her life.

The organization part, however, wasn't easy. She was usually late with her papers, but she loved the case method of learning, especially the courses on entrepreneurship. The sense of adventure, risk, and the chance to grow that entrepreneurialism offered thrilled her. But even then she lacked the ability to bring projects to completion. Her grades were not as good as her ability would have predicted.

Like Ashley, many entrepreneurs possess paradoxical pairs of traits, one of which leads to success, while the other can lead them to sabotage themselves (see table 3-1).

Not many people possess all of the qualities listed, but most entrepreneurs can see themselves in some of them. It's helpful to identify which apply to a given person so that person can zero in on controlling the negative side of the pair.

TABLE 3-1

Beneficial and problematic characteristics of idea hoppers

Beneficial	Problematic
Desire to be free and independent, master of own fate, own boss	Difficulty working on teams; trouble with intimacy in private life
Creative; constant new ideas	Impulsive
Initial surge of excitement	Excitement dissipates
Extremely hardworking	Driven, compulsive, maniacal
Ability to take risks	A need to be in danger in order to feel engaged and alive
Dreamer, visionary, pioneer	Trouble with implementation and sweating the details
Innovator	Can't or won't follow directions
Strong leader	Secretly harbors many self-doubts

To move forward, Ashley needed to figure out what force within her turned her away from a project once it got going. The modern world created the perfect storm for Ashley. Saved from her selfish mother by both her genes and her father, Ashley should have had the world by the tail . . . if only she could decide which tail! A born entrepreneur, Ashley was uniquely able to benefit from the opportunities that strew today's world, but at the same time, she found life to be a living hell, because she couldn't make up her mind.

What was in it for Ashley to stay stuck? Safety. Her shipwreck, to use Ortega y Gasset's term, which I'll explore closely in chapter 5, was largely the creation of her mother's selfishness, causing her enormous pain when she let herself feel it. So she avoided it and, in so doing, avoided growth.

Let me explain why her avoidance of the pain of her upbringing contributed to her indecisiveness. Ashley suffered with one of life's most crippling psychological disadvantages, a narcissistic parent, in Ashley's case, her mother, Daphne. When the little girl, Ashley, marshaled all her creativity and ambition and set up the best lemonade stand in the world, her mother beheld it as a threat, became jealous, and, behaving like the Medean monster she was, forced Ashley to take it down.

Despite the efforts of her good but usually absent father, Ashley never completely got over that trauma. While I've suggested that other issues, such as her conative style, contributed to her inability to get things done, her mother's cruelty and jealousy implanted in Ashley a deep fear of achieving . . . anything.

We worked together to revisit those years, see her mother for the primitive beast she was, defang her, bear the sadness and anger together, and then triumphantly and safely move on. This process of psycho-therapy was described by another legendary teacher of psychiatry at Harvard, the late Dr. Elvin Semrad. Semrad never wrote anything, but, as with Epictetus, his disciples passed along his various teachings in an oral tradition that continues to this day. Semrad summarized the three-step process Ashley and I went through: the therapist and client *acknowledge, bear, and put into perspective* powerful, painful feel-ings and memories. In so doing, the client grows and is able to lead a healthier life.

I also prodded Ashley to focus on what she wanted to do. Of the five elements of the basic plan, Ashley desperately needed element four, structure. To illustrate, imagine that Ashley was in my office. Here is how one of our conversations might have gone:

"I leave so many great ideas in the shower," Ashley tells me.

"You ought to keep a notebook hanging on a hook near the shower with a pen," I reply. "When you get out, write it down, or even step out of the shower for a moment and write it down while you're still wet. Then get back in. Or better yet, get one of those underwater writing boards scuba divers use and put it in your shower."

"Great idea," Ashley says. Then she pauses. "But then I'll have even more ideas I can't keep track of!"

"You've tried the obvious solutions?" I ask.

"Like what?" she asks.

"Like forcing yourself to work on only one idea."

"But that's just the problem. I can't decide which one."

"Then let me decide for you," I volunteer.

"How could you do that? Even if I agreed, you don't know what would be best for me."

"How do you know?"

"Because you're you and I'm me."

"OK," I say, "since you're the expert on you—and I agree that you are—tell me which one would be best for you?"

"I don't know! That's my dilemma. That's why I'm here."

"Then let me decide for you. Name ten ideas and I will pick the one for you to work on."

"Are you trying to upset me? What are you doing?" Ashley asks.

"I'm just taking your dilemma to the next logical step," I say. "If you can't decide, don't you think someone should? Why not me?"

"Because you don't know me well enough to know what would be best for me."

"Well, then, who does?" I ask.

"No one! That's just the point," Ashley says in exasperation.

"Well, if no one, including you, knows which idea you should pursue, then you've set it up so that you will stay awake at night following one idea after another, but you won't really go after any of them. Why would you want to do that?"

"I *don't* want to do that! That's why I'm here. I feel like we're playing 'Who's on first?' Can't you help me?"

"I've already offered to decide for you," I say. "That's much more than most shrinks would offer to do."

"But I don't want you to decide for me."

"So you've told me."

"So how do I decide?" she asks in genuine frustration.

"I believe you know," I said, trying my best not to anger her.

"Why would I *be* here if I knew?"

"Because you don't want to decide. You're using me as a dodge. You can say to yourself, 'Well, I've found a consultant to help me decide, an expert on helping people focus. He'll work it out for me.' And then you can keep on not deciding."

"You're telling me this is all a game?" she snaps back.

"Not a game. An act of self-deception. An act of self-sabotage. People do it all day long. Deceive themselves, sabotage themselves. We're all very good at it. I'm as good at it as you are, probably even better! It's part of being human."

"There's no pill for this?" Ashley asks. "I was really hoping for a pill."

"Everyone wants a pill. I've got nothing against pills. I'd want a pill if I were you, too. I prescribe pills all the time. But for the right conditions. What you have is not one of the right conditions. You have the problem of too many enthusiasms and not enough necessities."

"Yes," Ashley says.

"But sooner or later, you have to make a decision. Without a pill, without your husband or me or someone else doing it for you. You want like crazy to get out of doing it, but you know you can't. We can wait together; I'm glad to do that with you. Some people call that psycho-therapy, waiting together. There really is no hurry, but you do know deciding is what you have to do." I pause, then add with a smile, "Un-less, of course, you want me to decide for you."

"Why is this so difficult for me?" Ashley asks. "Am I afraid of something?"

"Sure you are. We all are. We'll come to that in good time. But, mean-while, you have to settle on something."

"So how do I do it? How do I settle?"

"Oh," I say, "there are lots of ways." And then I suggest various structures. "You've probably heard of them all. You make a list of all the possible contenders, and then you go down the list and rate each one on a scale from one to ten. Or, you go down the list and write down the pros and cons of each one. Or, you pick someone who knows you well and you brainstorm with her, going down the list. Or, you analyze which ones are most practical for you to do now. Or, if you are so inclined, you pray on it and see if God has any input for you. Or, you make a list of the possibilities in big block letters and put it on a wall you look at every day. That way you are trying to plant all the possibilities in your subconscious where they can swim around and see if one jumps out and grabs you as the lead contender. Or, you try hypnosis and see what comes out when you're in a trance. I'm not at all kidding; some people make important and good decisions that way. Or, you give yourself a deadline and say, 'I have to make a decision by noon next Friday,' or whenever, hoping panic will squeeze the right answer out of you. Or you go in the opposite direction and tell yourself not to think about these projects for two weeks, and if you can do that, you then see how you feel two weeks from now. Or you can get super-quantitative and assign numerical values to all the pros and cons of each project and then see which one emerges on top."

"Wow," Ashley says, "that's quite a list."

"Oh, I could come up with a dozen more ways to make the decision. A visual usually helps. If you can, make the list in big block letters, or draw a giant wheel and have each option be a spoke. Some kind of visual that allows you to see all the possibilities arranged together outside of your head. There's something about doing that that seems to help most people focus in a more balanced way on what they really want."

"So not just your average list?"

"Usually not," I say. "Your average list is too reminiscent of drudgery. You want to pep this up. Use colors. Use poster board. Use flashing lights if you can. Anything to trick your mind into telling you what it is that you really want."

"Trick my mind?" Ashley asks.

"Yes," I say. "You seduce your mind by making a game out of the problem, turning the solving of it into fun. Your mind is tricking you now into not making the decision. The afraid part of your mind likes indecision and so doesn't want to give up the secret."

"What secret?" Ashley asks.

"What you really want to do, of course!" I reply. "Do you see what I mean? You need to set something up that is more engrossing than tossing and turning in indecision. You've gotta outdo that indecisive performance with a better performance. Then you'll see what you want."

Working in parallel, we both created a relationship that allowed her feelings about her mother slowly to be acknowledged, borne, and put into perspective, while simultaneously doing the more practical work of sorting through options and settling on one or two. Her idea of the ship-wrecked, when it emerged, was simple, as such ideas almost always are. "*I want to succeed, and I am going to, goddamnit,*" she said one day. And she did.

As in previous chapters, I now summarize the dangers Ashley's idea hopping created, using the basic plan as an outline:

1. ENERGY. Ashley wore herself out hopping from idea to idea. She became the victim of her own enthusiasms.

2. EMOTION. She blamed herself constantly, creating a force field of negative energy that dragged her down.

3. ENGAGEMENT. Unable to engage with one idea or one project, she lived in an ongoing state of engagement and disengagement.

4. STRUCTURE. Her solution was to establish structure, but she was unable to create it on her own.

5. CONTROL. Her mind ran away with her, usurping control. Her mind controlled her, rather than Ashley controlling her mind.

WHAT TO DO ABOUT IT

10 tips for idea hoppers

---

1 Review the basic plan: energy, emotion, engagement, structure, control. Consider what you need more of. For most people who idea hop, the problem lies in element four: structure.

2 Write down your ideas. Then peruse the list to see where your brain lights up most brightly. If you can't decide, pick no more than three items.

3 Next, set up a structure to help you first decide and then implement. Look at the many possibilities I suggested to Ashley for ideas of structures that might help.

4 While doing this, also write down the various people who might be able to help you. Friends, professionals, colleagues, relatives, anyone who you feel could help and would want to help. This kind of problem responds best to a team effort.

5 Consult with an entrepreneur coach. One excellent firm is called Strategic Coach. Based in Toronto and led by Dan Sullivan and his wife, Babs, Strategic Coach has been helping entrepreneurs achieve their goals for decades. I know their work firsthand, but there are now many different kinds of executive coaching systems. What's important is to find a coach and a system that works for you, as no one system works for everyone. Just don't fall into the trap of believing you can do it all alone.

6 Reflect, with someone who knows you well and likes you, on what emotional obstacles or hot buttons might be getting in your way.

Are you like Ashley, fearing success because success got tangled up with feelings of danger when you were a child?

7 Stay in the game. Use your power. Don't pull back out of a fear of winning, of hurting the opposition. Many people so fear their own power that they pull back rather than use it full force. Sometimes people fear that in order to achieve a goal, they will somehow hurt someone else. Life is not a zero-sum game. Usually, when you achieve a goal, others benefit as well. Even if you win a direct competition, say, beat someone at tennis, your opponent, the loser of the match, also wins in that he gains valuable experience, may feel motivated to do better next time, may have picked up some pointers from you, and may have deepened a relationship with you. The cliché is correct: the only true losers are the ones who do not play.

8 Don't fall into the trap of selling yourself short. Most people possess more power than they use or give themselves credit for. One of the things I learned in my years of consulting to the Harvard chemistry department, a world-class group with five Nobel Prize winners on the faculty, is that most of the graduate students and post docs secretly feel as if they somehow sneaked into the program and didn't deserve to be there. Feeling inadequate is often just that, a feeling, not a fact. Side with the part of you that feels you can succeed. Gradually, that part of you will grow.

9 The old saying is correct: Whether you think you can or you think you can't, you're right. Along those lines, psychologist Carol Dweck has proven that a growth mind-set trumps a fixed mind-set. A growth mind-set says, "No matter what my goals may be, I can find the resources I need to achieve them." A fixed mind-set, on the other hand, says, "I am limited by my IQ, income, physical

appearance, ethnicity, gender, and every other quality I possess."
Dweck's research proves that both mind-sets are self-fulfilling
prophesies, and that anyone can learn and develop a growth
mind-set.[3] This is great news!

10 Celebrate your gift: you have many ideas. Just team up with the
right people—usually people who do not have many ideas but
are good at implementing others'—to see your ideas turn into
realities.

worrying

how to turn toxic worry into problem solving

Jack Rosenblum was already making his mental to-do list long before his alarm beeped at 4:30 a.m. He had scheduled a breakfast meeting at 7:30 with Marvin and had the regular call with Banyon at 11. Besides those two appointments, he had several phone calls to make and some research to squeeze in.

"Ugh," Jack said to himself as he remembered he had another damn lunch with Serena. They were supposed to discuss her proposal for a biotech investment. He hated having to eat with people he didn't particularly like talking to, but it came with the territory.

When the alarm went off, Jack's wife, Nan, grumbled loudly, put a pillow over her head, and turned over. He got out of bed and walked into their large bathroom. The first thing he did was to hit the brew button on the espresso machine stationed on the bathroom counter like a gas pump. Then he checked his messages.

"R U still on for squash?" read the text from Andy.

"Sorry, must cancel," Jack texted back. "Crazy busy."

"OK," Andy replied. "Hangover anyway. Back 2 bed. Later."

Jack put the phone down and turned on the shower. He was, in his own words, "one hyper dude." An up-and-coming hedge fund manager, Jack was always "on" and proud of it. He boasted that he'd trained himself over the years to function perfectly well on four hours of sleep a night.

When Nan pointed out that most human beings—herself included—needed more than that, he'd respond, "I can always sleep when I'm dead."

It was 5:15 when Nan, cranky and exhausted, came downstairs to the kitchen. She was angry at Jack for waking her up so early again. If he couldn't sleep himself, he could at least be considerate enough to go to the guest room. She felt like a zombie, and that she was married to one, too. She fought off a strong desire to yell at him.

Jack was already twenty minutes deep into the futures market on his laptop, which Nan snarkily referred to as his "binky." Staring at the screen, he was chewing the crusty nub of skin around his thumb again. It was an old, anxious habit he'd picked up in childhood from his father, and one that drove Nan crazy.

He was so engrossed in reading about yesterday's big market drop that he didn't look up as she made herself a cappuccino. She wondered how long it would take for him to notice that she was even in the room. Over the nine years of their marriage, the man Nan had thought of as her soul mate had transformed from a brilliant, fun-loving, All-American hockey player at Boston University into an anxious workaholic, a stereotypical Wall Street wheeler-dealer. She could barely recognize him anymore.

An efficient worker as a student, Jack had been able to party all night, then ace the stats exam the next day. Nine years and two kids later, Nan's once lovable boy-outta-Queens reminded her more of a cold-blooded financial shark, his eyes silently scanning for possible prey.

Jack believed he was enjoying himself. He felt something akin to joy while trolling for companies to invest in; when he closed a deal, the feeling reminded him of scoring a goal in hockey. There was that inner "whoop!" Even when he wasn't working, he loved to talk about

People who fit the category of ADT outlined in this chapter tend to agree with the following statements.

I worry even when external reality doesn't warrant worry.

No matter how hard I work, I always feel as if I haven't done enough.

The failing economy and the 3 billion new capitalists overseas make me worried all the time.

I come from a family of worriers.

I get anxious when I get close to success.

If I worried less, I'd be more successful.

I have trouble voicing my complaints at work.

I can't remember the last time I wasn't worried about something.

People who are not prepared annoy me.

Let's face it: the world is going to hell in a handbasket.

Too often, I hold back on life out of fear.

---

investments, buys, sells, and puts, and anything else related to making money, preferably lots of it at a time. He was obsessed by the game.

Of course, Nan understood how well she had benefited from Jack's Midas-like knack for making money. Though they had both come from humble backgrounds, they were now worth millions. They owned both a luxury condo on the Upper West Side and a summer house in the Hamptons, which Jack took to be the sine qua non of having "arrived" in New York. Their kids went to Manhattan private schools. They were known to outsiders as an "it" couple. But there was a steep price to pay for the marble bathrooms and chauffeurs, and it felt to Nan like it was getting steeper every day.

"Stop biting your thumb!" she snapped.

Caught in the act, Jack hastily dropped his blood-specked hand and kept staring at the screen.

Nan, remembering she valued compassion, decided again to try to connect. She went over to Jack and put her hands on his shoulders, gently massaging them while trying to turn him away from the screen. But instead of relaxing into her palms, she felt him tighten.

"Honey," she tried. "Please. What are you worried about now?"

He was always worrying about something.

"I'm planning," Jack said impatiently. "Our lives depend on it. How can I win if I'm not ahead of the pack?"

Nan felt the air leaving her, like a deflating balloon. She just didn't have the energy any more to try to save him or their relationship. Though they had more than enough money, his worries about their mythical "future" were both incessant and contagious. She and the kids felt his anxiety radiating from him like heat from an engine whenever he was around, and often even when he wasn't. If they tried to interrupt him, he would become defensive and snappish. The kids were only ages six and eight, but they had already learned to tiptoe around him. Nan's dream marriage and family had turned into a tense, unhappy quartet. She felt tired and beaten.

"Can you at least *try* to make it to Jeremy's play tonight?" Nan felt the squeaky, accusatory "try" make it into her voice before she could suppress it.

"Would he rather go to a school that puts on a play and have me not there?" Jack snapped. "Or would he prefer to go to crap school like I did and have me there at the play that never gets put on?"

Nan threw up her hands and screamed, "Stop it! Stop it! Stop living in your fucking childhood!"

Stunned, Jack was silent.

"*We* are your family now!" she shouted. "For all your father never made much money, he was there for you at four in the morning every day to get you out on the ice! He'd be ashamed of you if he knew how little time you spend with his grandkids!"

Nan had landed a body blow, for Jack's father had died, still a poor man, only a year before.

On the train to work, Jack buried the sting of his wife's words by checking his e-mail while listening to podcasts of business news. Constantly scanning for opportunities, he felt more anxious than usual. So he bit his thumb, scratched his head, drummed his fingers, and bounced his knee up and down, the molecules of anxiety now in full flow.

Jack understood that he had a problem. At Nan's insistence, he'd tried dealing with his chronic anxiety in some halfhearted ways. Couple's therapy and meditation were useless because he could not quiet down long enough to focus on them. He'd discontinued Prozac because it cut his sex drive. His failed attempts at getting help merely prodded him to work harder in his career. Working harder was his remedy for just about everything. "More" was always his target, never "enough."

He felt that if only he could earn more money, the anxiety would morph into confidence. So he resolved to be more disciplined, to work longer hours. Once he scored big, as he liked to say, he would spend more time at home, more time with Nan, more time with the kids.

After his grueling day, Jack came home to find the house lights off and Nan's car gone. "They should have been back from Jeremy's play by now," he thought. Wondering what had delayed them, he stepped into the kitchen and turned on the overhead lights. There on the cold marble counter, he found a note in his wife's handwriting:

Dear Jack,

I had such high hopes, such sweet dreams for us. If ever you decide you want to pursue them with me as we planned and promised, let me know. In the meantime, you're on your own. I've taken the kids to Annie's.

Jack was dumbstruck. For a moment, he felt nothing. Then, as if on cue, he opened his laptop to check the markets.

Jack's backstory

As is always the case, Jack's version of ADT originated both in his childhood and in the world in which he worked as an adult. Many thousands of adults today live with ongoing, preoccupying worry, such that paying attention is all but impossible. We live in an age of worry and fear, amplified by the instant transmission of bad news, so Jack's kind of ADT is common indeed.

His problem derived primarily from fear. Jack's genes were already packed with a predisposition to worry, but the Holocaust carried that familial predisposition to an extreme.

Jack came from a poor German-Jewish immigrant family. His grandfather, Josef, had survived Buchenwald as a child. Freed from near starvation and the horrors of the camp, Josef found his way to Queens in the 1940s, married an American girl from a close-knit Orthodox family, and fathered three children, including Jack's father. Josef worked for the city as a janitor for his entire working life. Though the family was poor, they were bound together through strict observance of their religion, and enjoyed being part of their synagogue community.

Life was a struggle for a man on a janitor's salary, and money was always an issue. Aside from trying to keep a perch on a lower rung of the middle-class American-dream ladder, the family was haunted by a constant feeling of dread. Social scientists have identified the subliminal but constant fear of death as a major impulse behind much human behavior. "Terror management theory" asserts that human beings—the only living beings that understand that they will die one day—do everything they can to escape the terror of death.[1] Religion provides one way of dealing with that fear, but people also turn to nationalism, drugs, hatred of others, and various other forms of psychological survivalism.

For European Jews facing extinction at the hands of the Nazis, terror management became a crucial tool in survival. To guard against the fear of annihilation, Josef and many like him developed a fear-based survivor mentality that translated into a survivalist's creed: "What doesn't kill you makes you stronger." For Josef, life was full of threats, and it was crucial to arm himself and his family against any attack, real or imagined.

When he was five years old, Jack once overheard his grandfather tell a neighbor what it was like in the camp—how he had killed and eaten a rat, and what it was like to see the gauzy ash dust of the victims spewing from the crematories. When Jack woke up screaming that night, his parents gave Josef strict orders to never talk about Buchenwald again, especially in Jack's presence.

As is the case with children whose familial background includes genocide, incest, alcoholism, drug addiction, and abuse, discussing this family's trauma—particularly with Josef—became absolutely taboo, because doing so brought forth too much pain. So Josef found other ways to teach his grandson about victimhood. One day, Josef played a "trust game" with Jack. He told Jack to walk up the stairway eight steps and then to fall backward. "I will catch you," Josef told Jack.

Jack obeyed, and Josef stood aside and made no effort to catch him. The little boy fell down the stairs and his head struck the floor. "That will teach you," he told the weeping boy. "Never trust anyone."

The lesson stuck. Early on, Jack learned—or was taught—that life is never safe. His upbringing taught him to depend on nothing and no one.

escape from anxiety

When he was roughly the same age, Jack's father, Daniel, had received the same lesson in distrust from Josef, and had likewise imprinted many of the issues of the trauma survivor.[2] Threat and victimhood echoed through Jack's family like the hum of a refrigerator, and Jack incorporated it without ever really hearing it, much less understanding it. He felt different from other kids in his Queens neighborhood, but didn't know why.

At the same time, Jack's parents stressed achievement. Daniel was a middle-school math teacher; Jack's mother, Ellen, a housewife. Though they had not been much better off financially than Josef, they did manage to see that Jack and his three siblings went to a decent public school, received Hebrew lessons, and enjoyed respectable, if not posh, bar and bat mitzvahs. Jack's father also saw to it that his son became a hockey jock. He would get Jack up at 4 a.m. to take him to practice. Thanks to a quick mind and an unexpected talent, Jack parlayed hockey into a college degree.

Hockey turned out to be a godsend, not only because it opened college doors, but also because it loosened Jack up, at least for a while. He discovered, or rather developed, a fun-loving side. He won a coveted hockey scholarship to Boston University, which had one of the best hockey programs in the United States. At BU, he felt, for the first time in his life, an escape from dread. The new part of him took shape on the ice and in the dorms on Commonwealth Avenue. He made friends with people from diverse backgrounds who did not carry the assumption that the world was a dark and fearful place. He discovered people who could actually be counted on; he learned that, once in a while, it was safe to let down his guard.

Jack opened up enough to let love in. Indeed, he fell head over heels in love. It happened sophomore year, and in the way love usually does happen—randomly on purpose. It happened with Nan because, as Jack liked to say, "she was the prettiest girl in the room that night."

Nan's family was very different from Jack's. Hers was a happy, middle-class Jewish family from Wellesley, Massachusetts. She was a bright and serious English major, with a minor in musical performance. Jack sought out and brought out her inner animal. Not committed to a career, Nan dreamed most of all of creating a close-knit family, full of fun, love, and celebrations. She thought Jack was even smarter than she was. She also sensed the wounded boy inside the powerful jock, the insecure man inside the carousing party animal.

When she would chide him about his sexist attitude about her large, maternal, "Gawazanga!" breasts, he'd tease her back. "Sorry, honey, but I'm just a dumb jock. For me, it's all about sex." She'd punch him in the arm, and they'd go back to bed and make love and be happy. Like the incipient Jewish mother she was, she scooped Jack up like a stray puppy and loved him into something akin to mental health. Without Jack being aware he was doing so, he opened up to Nan. He told about the cruel trick his grandfather played on him on the stairwell, the paranoia of his childhood, and the shadow always hovering over his family. Nan listened, took it all in, washed it out, and gave it back to Jack with the most comfortable, trusting words of all: "I love you."

They had big, bold dreams of a happy family, "with none of the crap I grew up with," Jack would say.

displaced dread

But once Jack got the job at Goldman Sachs, and subsequently left Goldman to start his own hedge fund, his anxiety genes fired up with a vengeance. Compensating for the fact that he'd grown up in a family without much money, he doubled down to make it. Mortified by their small, dowdy house and old furnishings, he tried many times to give his parents money so that his father could quit working. But Daniel always rejected his son's offer, saying, "I like what I do. If you're ashamed of me, I'm sorry."

"Dad," Jack protested, "I'm the opposite of ashamed of you. I'd just like to pay you back for all you did for me."

"Then be a good man and lead a happy life," Daniel said. "That's all I want."

"You don't think I'm doing that?" Jack asked.

"You tell *me*," Daniel replied.

That's where the conversation ended. The cryptic "you tell *me*" just hung in the air.

Daniel felt that to take his son's money would be to collude in an irreligious, workaholic lifestyle of which he disapproved. Once, when Daniel scolded Jack on this score, they had wound up not speaking to each other for two months.

"You pay too much attention to your work and not enough to your family," Daniel had chided. "For all the money you make, God knows you're not living your life the right way."

"Well, I'm making up for all the money you didn't make," came Jack's stinging reply. "At least . . . " Jack didn't say the rest of what he was thinking: "At least I make enough money to give my family a really good life."

Injured, the two of them retreated into a chillier relationship.

With no ice to skate on any longer, no locker-room culture to buoy him up, no college buddies to drink with, Jack retreated into himself, which soon devolved into a hyper, driven, anxious person. Instead of reaching out to Nan, he behaved as if she weren't there, much as Josef had taught him to do. He decided that college had been fantasyland. In the "real world," as he called it, dog ate dog, and trusting someone resulted in getting eaten.

The roller-coaster life of a hedge fund manager filled Jack with worry that coursed through his blood. But because he could not understand how anxiety was crippling him, he embraced it; he felt naked and vulnerable without it. He believed in the common, albeit crazy, notion that if he were bold enough to enjoy a worry-free moment, fate, like Josef, would let him fall down the stairs. But if he worried enough, fate would keep him safe.

If Nan or a friend ever tried to remind him that he should take a break or chill out for a weekend at the house in the Hamptons, he would ignore them. For Jack, family vacations were always "workations." Even when biking with the family, his mind was always on the markets. When he wasn't working, Jack truly didn't know what to do with himself. He felt something was wrong—that he was missing something or that he was near failure.

worry-holism

Jack could not see how fundamentally unhappy he was, and how unhappy he was making those around him. He thought he was on top of the world, but his anxiety led him to behave in precisely the wrong ways. He isolated himself and grew increasingly distant from Nan. Convinced that he was serving their shared dream of creating the happy family, he lost the central focus of their family life together.

All but addicted to toxic worry, Jack played a psychological trick on himself. He decided to think of his anxiety as something positive; he only felt comfortable when he was riveted to some worry or another. Without the painful comfort of anxiety, he felt vulnerable. So he courted worry as pain of worry focused him. So intense was his desire to achieve, and so intense was his fear of the consequences of not achieving at the very highest levels, that he felt compelled to throw himself into work completely and arm himself by anticipating everything that could possibly go wrong. Afraid to feel the real pain of how empty his life was becoming, he redoubled his focus on work.

While Nan looked on with growing dismay and finally distance, she gradually lost her ability to scoop him up and hold him. He'd grown too big and too powerful to hold, too fixed in his view of the world as a punishing, dangerous place. For a while she hoped she could bring back the man she'd fallen in love with, until that morning when hope went dark and she left.

Toxic worry—the tendency to focus excessively on problems that aren't all that important—is common in the millions of people today who perceive all the dangers in life but lose sight of the positive. They are driven to distraction by worry. This problem is so prevalent that I wrote a book about it (*Worry: Hope and Help for a Common Condition*, published in 1998). Since then, due to various modern issues I've mentioned, the problem of toxic worry has mushroomed. It's become our ambient noise.

Jack's tendency to worry had a genetic origin, exacerbated by the environment he chose to work in. Over the past twenty years, research has revealed a basis in our DNA for all moods and emotions, including worry.[3] Jack was born with anxiety genes. Scientists have identified a genetic variant that contributes to a heightened susceptibility to environmental stress of the kind his father and grandfather experienced. In addition, another genetic variant can create an inborn susceptibility to the negative moods Jack all but courted.

It has long been known that depression and toxic worry can spring from a genetically inherited lack of the powerful mood-stabilizing neurotransmitter, serotonin, in the brain.[4] Hence, the most commonly used medications to treat depression and anxiety, called selective serotonin reuptake inhibitors or SSRIs, raise serotonin levels in the brain.[5]

But genes never tell the entire story. Even a trait as highly inheritable as height also depends upon environment. If you grow up in a dungeon and never see the sun, or if you eat a meager diet, you will never grow as tall as your genes otherwise could help you to grow.

Jack was trained to worry. His grandfather tricked Daniel and Jack in a way that most would condemn as child abuse. But Josef thought he was doing them a favor. "That'll teach you! Never trust anyone. Not even the father and grandfather whom you love."

The psychological damage of Josef's trick, and the worldview the family held in general, produced in both Jack and his father the emotional equivalent of growing up in a dungeon, never seeing the light of day. Jack's genes combined with his experience to create a toxic worrier. Fortunately, environment intervened in a positive way when Jack got to BU. Under the influence of new friends, the hockey team, and removed from the dark influence of his father and grandfather, Jack learned to trust, to have fun, and even to fall in love.

But later on, environment intervened a third time, when Jack found himself in the competitive world of Wall Street. Josef's terrible lesson surged back into Jack's mind, as his primitive brain allowed his genetic tendencies to rule his world.

worry and "connected isolation"

Millions of people share Jack's genetic predisposition to worry. But not all of these millions worry in such a toxic way. Because Jack believed he needed his worrying to achieve at the highest levels, he turned it in his mind into an asset, even a state he thought of as weirdly pleasurable.

Modern life has created the conditions to draw out the toxic worry in anyone so predisposed. While a few fortunate people are equipped with "happy" genes that allow them virtually never to worry, and a few people are born cool as cucumbers and are destined to never get rattled, I've found that far more share Jack's genetic makeup.

Furthermore, various elements in today's world, and in the human psyche, combine in the perfect storm of toxic worry. Today's electronic communications technology assists the worry-o-genic forces, because it lets us saturate ourselves in bad news that is both instantaneous and constant. While none of us wants to hear bad news all the time, it grabs our attention much more quickly than good news and is always in plentiful supply. Life will never run out of bad news. And fear sells. There's big money in fear. Advertisers pay for eyeballs, and nothing captures a person's attention quicker than fear. Fear even beats sex. Hence, legions of creative people are committed to unearthing and distributing as much fear-fraught information as possible.

Most important of all, we are living in a time of a unique paradox that I mentioned in the introduction. While electronics connect us more than ever before in human history—indeed, electronic connection is this era's defining and crowning achievement—we've been disconnecting interpersonally. We are losing sight of each other, literally. People don't talk face-to-face as much as they did twenty years ago. As Harvard sociologist Robert Putnam documented in his prescient 2001 book, *Bowling Alone: The Collapse and Revival of American Community*, and MIT sociologist and psychologist Sherry Turkle explained in her 2012 book, *Alone Together: Why We Expect More from Technology and Less from Each Other*, we tend to live in a state of what I call "connected isolation."

Connected isolation is my ironic term for the common syndrome we see today in which people are connecting with each other and the world to the point of saturation—primarily through electronics—while suffering from a mounting, inchoate feeling of being more alone than they'd like to be. The modern state of connected isolation deprives people of the most powerful antianxiety agent ever developed: the human connection. (My old teacher of psychiatry, Harvard professor Thomas Gutheil, used to tell us, "It is fine to worry, even good to worry. Just never worry alone." Those words, *never worry alone*, have guided me ever since.)

One of the major reasons our era produces so much toxic worry is that too many people, like Jack, are worrying alone. Any latent tendency they might have toward toxic worry is activated by the world in which we live.[6] Table 4-1 shows how a beneficial, adaptive behavior like constructive worry can also become problematic with undiagnosed peripheral focus.

Jack was not incorrect in assuming that today's world is dangerous, and that there is plenty to worry about. Life is maddeningly uncertain. Trusting anyone is risky. Downsizing, outsourcing, and lawsuits abound.

TABLE 4-1

Beneficial and problematic characteristics of worriers

Beneficial	Problematic
Problem solving	Problem fixation
Responsible, conscientious	Hyper-vigilant
Ambitious, hardworking	Unable to relax and have fun
Self-reliant	Inability to trust; isolation
Focused	Obsessive
Scans for opportunity	Scans for threat
Protective	Paranoid
Competitive; enjoys high-pressure environments	Easily bored when not under high pressure

The economy is tenuous, and global competition can make anyone feel insecure.

But Jack worried far more than most people, and in a self-destructive fashion. He believed his worrying carried him to safety, while in fact it was distracting him from what really mattered.

Jack came to see me when he began to feel deeply enough the pain of losing Nan and the kids. In working with him, I validated his legitimate worries, but then asked him to look at how he amplified and exaggerated them and pointed out how he was crippling himself with his habitual toxic worry. Since one of the best remedies for toxic worry is never to worry alone, I joined Jack in his worrying but tried to cast it in a less menacing light.

I also probed Jack about why he held on to worry so tenaciously. "Why not let it go?"

"For the same reason I wouldn't walk naked down Fifth Avenue."

"You think your worrying protects you."

"I *know* it protects me."

"It hurts you more than you realize."

"How do *you* know?"

"Because I can see what you can't see."

"You're that smart?"

"No, you're that blind."

"You think I'm stupid?"

"No, in fact, I know you are brilliant. But you are blinded by what happened to you growing up, and what happened to your grandfather."

He held on to worry, ironically, to create a feeling of safety. Only by living in a state of constant fear could he feel safe. I worked with him to raise this insight to the level of conscious awareness and help him test the waters of adult life long enough find out that it is safe not to live in constant fear. That took some time.

Jack was also someone for whom I prescribed hefty daily doses of human connection as well as physical exercise. In addition, he benefited from the selective serotonin reuptake inhibitor, Lexapro. In general, these types of medications are vastly overprescribed, but Jack's worrying was so ingrained and toxic that medication, in combination with the other interventions, was indicated. It sped up the process toward health.

He was shipwrecked but didn't know it. I had to play the role of the fool with him and whisper in his ear what he did not want to hear.

"You miss Nan and your kids."

"Is that a question?"

"No."

"You're a son of a bitch," he said.

"You're a son of a bitch," I replied.

Long pause. Deep sigh. More silence.

"I really don't like you," he said.

"I don't blame you. I wouldn't like someone who showed me my mistakes either."

Long pause. Another deep sigh. "This sucks. I'm done with this." With that, Jack got up and left, his time far from up.

At the appointed time, the following week, he came back. And kept coming back until he learned how to change.

Successful resolution of ADT caused by toxic worry can happen. Especially when someone works as hard at solving the problem as Jack.

As I did with Les, Jean, and Ashley, I apply the basic plan to Jack's situation and note the following dangers:

1. ENERGY. Worry and chronic anxiety drain mental energy much as an open window in winter drains heat from the house. Bringing worry under control automatically boosts mental energy.

2. EMOTION. Emotion is the on-off switch for learning and peak performance. Toxic worry and chronic anxiety disable learning and prevent peak performance.

3. ENGAGEMENT. It's impossible fully to engage if worry preoccupies a piece of your mind.

4. STRUCTURE. If you are intensely worried, it becomes difficult to submit to the discipline of any structure. You keep drifting back to your worry, as your tongue to a canker sore.

5. CONTROL. In toxic worry, you give over control to the process of worrying.

WHAT TO DO ABOUT IT
10 tips for dealing with toxic worry

1. Never worry alone. Toxic worry feasts on a solitary victim, but flees when two or more join together.

2. Get the facts. Toxic worry is rooted in lack of information, wrong information, or both.

3   Make a plan. Toxic worry loves a passive victim, but cowers in the face of a person with a plan.

4   If the plan doesn't work, revise the plan. That's what life is all about, revising plans that don't work.

5   Bring in the right experts. They're usually worth what they cost.

6   Regular physical exercise helps your brain reject toxic worry.

7   Meditation is also a superb shield against toxic worry.

8   Divert yourself by doing something totally unrelated to what you are worrying about.

9   Keep perspective. Remember how much you've worried about in your life and how little of it actually came to pass.

10 Work on what I call "the basic equation of worry"—increased feelings of vulnerability combined with decreased feelings of power and control lead to toxic worry. So, anything that diminishes your feelings of vulnerability or increases your feelings of power and control will reduce toxic worry.

playing the hero

how to stop fixing everyone's problems—except your own

"How would your morale be if I fired all of you right now?" Stan yelled, his hands in fists, his face ablaze. The room went dead silent. Everyone stared at him.

"Morale is now a luxury we can't afford!" he shouted. "So let me invite you to shut up and go back to work before more people get fired."

Stunned, the staff silently stood up and filed out of the conference room. In the hallway on the way back to their cubicles, they shook their heads and exchanged glances that said, "Can you believe *that?*"

Stan remained standing in the room, not moving, his palms now flat on the conference table, his face in a fixed stare. Mary, the corporate vice president next to him, remained seated, saying nothing.

Unlike everyone else on the staff, Mary felt her heart go out to Stan. She always sensed his moods. Though he was brilliant, he was also arrogant and not psychologically astute enough to understand the origins of such fulminant rage.

Like Mary, he had been at the company for a long time. But now the organization was in transition, and Stan was taking the brunt of the pressure from the interim CEO, which Mary knew he was ill equipped to handle. Rather than accept and manage the pressure, Stan started to attack the people who worked for him.

"We're all under pressure, Stan," she ventured quietly.

Stan shot his gaze over to her. "Well, obviously," he snapped.

Mary believed she saw his eyes soften a little bit. She stood up and walked out into the hallway. She noticed that several people on the staff had doubled up in each other's cubicles, talking under their breaths. When she returned to her desk, Jennifer, the director of the northwest division, was waiting for her.

"What the hell was that about?" Jennifer asked. "All I did was mention that morale has dropped. It's obvious to everyone. Why can't he deal with it? Doesn't he understand that we've all been on pins and needles waiting for this new CEO to show up?"

"Yes, that was far from helpful," Mary said soothingly, "but I can't blame him for feeling frustrated. He's been under a huge amount of pressure. He's been trying as hard as he can to do what's being asked of him, but now he's managing from the bottom up and from the top down. He's feeling squeezed in the middle. If you think about it, it's no wonder his fuse is short."

"Well, so is everyone else's," Jennifer retorted. "He should start acting like a real manager and not like some foot-stomping five-year-old child." Then she leaned over and said to Mary in a serious tone: "Competent people have been fired around here for no reason other than to make room for the new CEO's buddies. This environment has become untenable. I've had enough."

People who fit the category of ADT outlined in this chapter tend to agree with the following statements.

I take on other people's problems at work as if they were my own.

When I see someone at work in distress, I feel instantly compelled to help that person.

I grew up taking care of people.

It's just not right to see someone struggle at work and not do your best to help out.

I am too soft-hearted.

I take on other people's problems too easily.

People tell me I should be more selfish.

I don't understand how anyone can say no when the job has to get done.

I hate the phrase, "Nice guys finish last."

Guilt is a big problem for me.

Then she handed Mary an envelope. "I've found another job. I'm handing in my resignation, effective two weeks from today."

When Mary first took the job back in the mid-1990s, she could not have been happier. Landing the position shortly after graduating from business school, she learned fast. She was dogged, curious, and worked hard. Her instincts were sharp. Rising from her starting position as a marketing manager, she quickly climbed the ladder to become the head of corporate communications. The staff she worked with was dedicated, tight-knit, and well paid, and they all respected one another.

Then, beginning with 9/11, the recession that followed, and the implosion of the dot-com technology business, things began to slowly come apart. Big retailers began closing their doors. Annual bonuses shrank. And dollars dried up. The CEO, the bean counters, and HR began pecking away at marketing resources, insisting on cutting back on everything from travel expenses to administrative assistants to copy paper. Mary found that she and the others in corporate were having to work harder and longer with less support than ever.

When the news came down that the company had been bought by a much larger competitor, the insidious merger and acquisition process began. Partners and managers from a large consultancy made their appearance. People began to avoid spontaneous conversation; they only talked to each other behind closed doors. Cliques formed; gossip about office politics spread like weeds where it had never grown before. Hank, the revered CEO, was let go, pending the hiring of a new CEO recommended by the consulting firm guiding the merger.

While people waited for the new man to arrive on the scene, more gossip spread. Would the new CEO clean house? Morale continued to plummet. People started losing interest in their jobs and worked half-heartedly, though they dared not come in late or leave early for fear of being singled out. They stayed at their desks, lackluster, unable to focus. Their bodies were present, but their minds were usually elsewhere.

Every few hours, some colleague, wanting to share the latest gossip or cry on Mary's shoulder, would tap on the glass of her office door. She would sigh and wave the person in. She never even considered waving anyone away. After all, she was the staff's mother hen, a role she had played for years.

Like Jennifer, Mary had begun sniffing around for other corporate communications jobs, but even the ones in faraway places were well below her level of expertise and pay scale. Besides, she couldn't quit: she brought in money her family depended on. Her husband, a self-employed contractor, didn't earn nearly enough to cover all their expenses. And since her son suffered from chronic asthma that often demanded trips to the emergency room, they depended on the medical benefits she got from her employer.

Every day, she came home feeling more and more exhausted and worried. She and Doug, her husband, would argue. "Look, you're miserable and you're making us miserable," he would say. "Why don't you quit? You could go to work for a smaller company. You could do PR. Heck, you used to wait tables. Anything would be better than this."

That pushback, of course, made her hit the roof. "I've spent my whole life in management. I'm good at my job. I'm not about to leave now and go wait tables. How could you even suggest that? It's like me saying, 'Why don't you take a job mowing lawns?'"

altruism and the curse of the toxic handler

Conventional wisdom, traditional psychology, and the laws of economics tell us that people act according to their own self-interest. Once pretense and hypocrisy get stripped away, each of us is wired to push others aside to get what we want. Humans are fundamentally selfish, or so the party line has it.

In addition, our current era actually encourages selfishness, even glorifies it; narcissism is in its heyday, on full display everywhere. First identified as a moniker for modern life by Christopher Lasch in 1979, the narcissist has only grown more common since.[1] Our current zeitgeist, or at least a portion of it, treats selfishness as a bona fide virtue. Gordon Gekko's line from the 1987 film *Wall Street* seems even more applicable today than then: "Greed is good!"

Everywhere you go, you find talented takers who are all about themselves: the doltish, self-aggrandizing athlete or hip-hop star; the CEO who pockets an unconscionable salary while refusing to offer health benefits to hourly workers; the entertainer who bathes in money while refusing to pay minimal child support; the entrepreneur who brags about his ability to get people to waste money on goods they can't afford and will never use.

Then there are the people who can't help it—those who just seem to lack the DNA for empathy. Such folks seem untroubled by and often unaware of the suffering they cause by playing politics and stabbing backs. In the close quarters of departments and teams, such toxic people can poison their organizations. As reporter, author, and social commentator Marie Brenner has said, "Narcissism is the polio of our era."[2] We have no vaccine on the horizon.

Some would argue that even deeds that seem the most altruistic are selfish, deriving from an innate desire to serve oneself.[3] However, recent research suggests otherwise. It appears that some altruistic behaviors are built into certain species. The most spectacular examples come from ants, "the other conqueror of the earth," as Harvard biologist and naturalist E. O. Wilson dubs these creatures, which are a million times more abundant than humans.

Some species of ants routinely take on tasks that lead them to die sooner than other ants.[4] The ant's altruism is genetically determined and irresistible. Free will does not factor in. While humans seem to possess some degree of free will (with a nod to the absolute determinists who insist we don't possess one iota), recent research shows that we sometimes choose to act against our selfish desires, sharing more with the ant than we realize.

Many humans, while equipped with the ability to decide between a selfish goal and an altruistic goal, are genetically wired to focus their attention more on the needs of others than their own. A study in 2005 by Rachel Bachner-Melman and others used a questionnaire assessing "the propensity to ignore one's own needs and serve the needs of others." Based on responses from 354 families, Bachner-Melman concluded that "the genetic architecture of altruism in humans is partly built from genes that drive an altruistic behavioral pattern regardless of kin considerations."[5] In other words, some people do have altruism built into their DNA.

To satisfy the cynic, we can say that for the altruist, helping other people is pleasurable. As is usually the case from a neurotransmitter standpoint, the key player is dopamine. A squirt of dopamine gives you pleasure. The drug addict is an addict because he's found that his drug gives him that squirt. But the altruist may be an altruist for the very same reason. Doing something for someone else raises the dopamine level.

Now that we can watch in real time the activity of the pleasure centers of the brain through functional magnetic resonance imaging (fMRI), it's possible to assess at the cellular level how much pleasure a person is feeling. In one clever experiment, Jorge Moll and colleagues scanned subjects while they were making decisions involving charitable giving. In some instances, the subjects were asked if they'd accept money for themselves. Of course, they accepted the money and the fMRI registered pleasure. But then they were asked to give 40 percent of what they were to receive to a charity. On the fMRI, those who chose to give the money away registered even more intense activity in the pleasure centers than when they received money for themselves.[6] Hence we see a biological basis for the words in the prayer of Saint Francis of Assisi, "It is in giving that we receive."[7]

Enter Mary, wired to be altruistic. Using her inborn altruism, Mary handles toxic people like Stan with grace and skill. Coining the term "toxic handler" in 1999, Peter Frost and Sandra Robinson described the person who mediates between a toxic individual, typically in a high-power position, and the rest of the world.[8] Some examples: the prima donna's agent, who absorbs her abuse before it can do too much damage to her public image; the superstar athlete's crony on the team, who makes excuses for him to the world; the loyal lieutenant to the talented but arrogant CEO, who mops up the blood spilled day after day and bandages up the victims; the loyal grandson of the tyrannical mater familias, who finds ways to excuse his grandmother's contemptibly cruel words and deeds; or the right-hand man of the take-no-prisoners crime boss, whose job it is to make murder look like suicide.

Hugely valuable in organizations of all kinds, as well as in families, toxic handlers like Mary save the group and its mission. While these people can't prevent the ongoing, poisonous behavior of the individual they are handling, they prevent the poison from spreading too far. Without their interventions, the work of the group—whatever group it might be—would be jeopardized, if not destroyed.

Where does such a valuable asset, a toxic handler, come from? I'm tempted, because of all the good they do, to say from heaven, but such an explanation won't do because it is also the case that, as much good as these people do, they also can cause great pain to themselves and those close to them.

While toxic handlers save souls, they also tend to wrestle with a unique set of internal issues. Psychological jargon dismisses toxic handlers as codependent, or victims of the so-called "Stockholm syndrome." I don't like using these terms because they are entirely pejorative, and so leave out the positives, but certain elements of codependency and the Stockholm syndrome do apply to people like Mary. Mary could be defined as a "vicarious codependent." She lives through the people she helps. She gains satisfaction in helping others reach the limelight, while avoiding the limelight herself. In my experience, women are more prone to this pattern than men. Perhaps due to how they are socialized, many women feel skittish about taking center stage, so they use their wits to help other people get their names on the marquee.

Indeed, it may be a male value to put more emphasis on individual achievement than on facilitating others' achievements. Who's to say which is better—being the star or being the one who made the star a star?

Traditional (male, psychoanalytic) psychology regards the backing away from center stage as weak, guilt-driven, fearful, and altogether neurotic (an obsolescent term itself), while taking center stage as strong, confident, bold, and altogether healthy. But such traditional psychology (I could really say old-fashioned and outdated psychology) overly pathologizes humility, generosity, the desire to nurture and protect, and the overarching wish to connect rather than to achieve. Neither way is better. I believe it is important rather to acknowledge both ways as potentially healthy as well as potentially harmful.

For example, the humble, nurturing connector can become what is called, in the jargon, "codependent," and can go to extremes, which is the case with the Stockholm syndrome. The Stockholm syndrome refers to the bizarre and thoroughly counterintuitive reversal of the hostility that hostages initially feel toward their captors. Rather than hate them, over time they can come to admire them and want to stay with them. The syndrome is named after a 1973 bank robbery in Stockholm, Sweden, where several bank employees were held hostage in the bank's vault for six days. To everyone's astonishment, the victims allied with their captors to such an extent that they refused help from the outside. Once the ordeal ended, the hostages actually defended their captors.

What went on in that bank vault is actually as old as human nature itself, and was given a name decades before the Stockholm bank job. In her classic 1936 book, *The Ego and the Mechanisms of Defense*, Anna Freud, Sigmund's daughter, described what she called a "defense mechanism," a form of psychological self-protection to which desperate people sometimes unconsciously resort in traumatic situations.

Anna Freud, who psychoanalyzed children, suggested that by "identifying with the aggressor," as she put it, a child defends himself against feelings of helplessness and vulnerability.[9] The child identifies with and wants to remain close to the person who threatens him. In a breathtaking, utterly counterintuitive reversal for which the unconscious is famous, hostility magically becomes a desire to affiliate.

As Anna Freud put it, "By impersonating the aggressor, assuming his attributes or imitating his aggression, the child transforms himself from the person threatened into the person who makes the threat."[10] Freud was writing about her observations in the development of the superego of children, but adults also can use the same defense mechanism she so aptly named "identification with the aggressor."

In its more generalized form, Anna Freud, and psychoanalysts since, called this defense mechanism "reaction formation." In using reaction formation, the individual unconsciously defends against unacceptable feelings by consciously espousing their opposite.

The most famous example in English literature is when Queen Gertrude speaks the line in the third act of *Hamlet*, "The lady doth protest too much, methinks." In the play within the play, designed by Hamlet to catch the conscience of the king, the fictional queen promises, should her husband die, never to marry again. Her promises betray to the perceptive Gertrude a desire to do precisely the opposite, as Gertrude herself did.

Using such reaction formation, we see people who fear their own homosexual yearnings viciously condemning homosexuality; people who lack religious faith fiercely condemning nonbelievers; people who actually hate another person professing love for that person; people who harbor toxic envy condemning envy as a deadly sin; people who yearn to be rich condemning the wealthy; people who roil with sexual feelings condemning the life of the flesh; people who are titanically ambitious insisting they are content with what they have; people who feel wild rage professing equanimity; people who seek to kill professing pacifism.

The difference between hypocrisy and reaction formation lies in the role of the unconscious. The hypocrite knows he is lying. But the person using reaction formation consciously believes he's a pacifist, while his unconscious steams with a desire to murder every day.

Mary's backstory

Mary's version of ADT is most common among our kindest people, the people who truly want to help others even before helping themselves. Modern life, with its instant access to everything, makes it easier than ever to investigate and try to solve everyone else's problems.

Aside from her DNA, Mary's skill as a toxic handler got its start in her family of origin. Her mother, Flannery, was a shy, devoutly Catholic violinist. She fell in love with an up-and-coming conductor named Devon David while studying at Tanglewood, the summer home of the Boston Symphony orchestra, when they were both in their early twenties.

Flannery thought she'd gone to heaven when Devon paid attention to her. The cognoscenti at Tanglewood dubbed him "the next Lenny," giving him the affectionate nickname they reserved for their darling, Leonard Bernstein. Devon's star shined as bright as a star could shine that summer. That he was an avid womanizer and an obvious narcissist didn't bother Flannery in the least. She lived for his glances, his touch, his kiss. Devon simply and effortlessly swept her away.

Their marriage produced three children in four years. Flannery gave up her career as a musician in order to take care of the kids, giving Devon the freedom he needed to fly high and keep up with a blistering concert schedule, which he gloried in. Like most narcissistic men, Devon flew into cataclysmic rages whenever he imagined himself slighted, diminished, ignored, or disobeyed. Devon routinely arrived home ready to attack. A concert had one flaw, a flutist missed a note, one of two sons had left a toy in the foyer— any trigger could set him off. When he raged, words quickly gave way to slaps and shoves, objects thrown, beatings, and sometimes blood.

No one dared do anything until Mary got old enough to get involved, which was at the age of four. The eldest child, Mary learned to protect her siblings and her mother, first by cleverly learning her father's moves. She instinctively knew the semaphore that announced impending rage. A raised eyebrow, glasses being cleaned, a clearing of the throat at a certain higher pitch, a twitch of the left ring finger, an ever so slight decrease in volume of voice, a tiny shift in cadence in asking, "What did you say?" or even, "How was your day?"—any of these and many more could portend an eruption, which Mary learned to anticipate.

Even as she learned the warning signals, this gifted child also learned the art of defusing her father's rage. She learned that her daddy loved to be hugged about the waist, but not held by the hand. She learned that daddy would calm down if Mary did a cartwheel on the living room rug, but that he hated it if she struck a wrong note on the piano. She learned that he liked to hear her say, "I love you," but that he hated to be asked a question or be asked to do something. And as she got older, Mary's mother made her swear not to speak of the women Devon paraded around town with.

Mary also learned, at age five, how to be Devon's bartender. When he asked her to make him a drink, she would get ice from the freezer, put it into the right crystal glass, pour Scotch on top of the ice, and add just the right amount of soda water. At age six, she learned how to make a Martini, "up, with a twist." Not many six-year-olds develop the skill of peeling a sliver off the rind of a lemon, rubbing it on the rim of the mar-tini glass, and twisting its essence into the drink. But even more remark-ably, she learned, most tactfully, how to regulate his intake so the alcohol would work its desired effect, which was to put him to sleep before he became violent.

She couldn't have told you, if you'd asked her, how she managed to do all this, but she did it every day that he was at home. No one ever men-tioned this life-saving talent of hers. Her mother and brothers sensed that to do so risked her father seeing through Mary's tricks, which would have resulted in devastation. Accordingly, they pretended they didn't see the magic Mary worked. Flannery had no doubt whatsoever but that God had given Mary this gift to mollify the devil in Devon, and thanked God and her daughter in her nightly prayers.

When Mary went off to college, the family held its collective breath in terror. But fate intervened. Devon suffered a hemorrhagic stroke that left him paralyzed. He was no longer able to conduct—or to assault.

the toll of toxic handling

Mary's early wounds inflicted by her malignantly narcissistic father led her to become a woman with enormous generosity and power to heal others. Year after year, Mary practiced her unique art, gradually raising it to a rare skill indeed—a skill she was able to transfer into her handling of other people, outside of home. Compared to her father, most other toxic people were easy to deal with. Her handling of Stan was just one in a long line of triumphant examples.

But such triumph came at a price. Without realizing it, Mary gave too much of herself over to the well-being of Stan and the people she worked with. She lost the focus she needed to do her own job well, not to mention to care for her own family.

Finding herself increasingly depressed and burnt out, she began feeling less and less well physically, despite her efforts to keep up with her regular gym visits. Her neck and shoulders hurt constantly; she had more and more trouble sleeping. Her doctor prescribed Prozac and referred her to a therapist. After a few weeks, Mary began to feel the effects of the Prozac. They muffled her fragile emotions a bit, but she lost all her sexual desire. She felt the Prozac made her less mentally alert. She never followed through with the therapist, but her doctor refilled her prescription and urged her to take it, saying that the drug was safe and effective.

At least, the doctor reassured her, "It's something." Sadly, she needed far more than that something.

In today's world, bursting with conflict and narcissism, altruists like Mary often absorb and neutralize the poisons. They don't realize how at risk they are putting themselves and others. As I've suggested, women fall into this trap of self-sabotage through self-sacrifice more easily than men do, but kind and generous people of both sexes in any walk of life are susceptible to it.

Table 5-1 offers companion pairs of beneficial and problematic qualities in toxic handlers.

TABLE 5-1

Beneficial and problematic characteristics of toxic handlers

Beneficial	Problematic
Sensitive; perceives emotional conflicts others often miss	Easily hurt; sometimes perceives slights where none intended
Hates to offend or hurt another person in even a minor way	Trouble being candid and frank
Eager to help resolve conflict	Difficulty dealing with tension of conflict long enough for full disclosure
Able to reframe a situation in a positive or at least less negative light	Has a touch of Pollyanna
Nonjudgmental; sees every nuance	Trouble judging others when critical appraisal needed
Earns the trust and gratitude of most people	Has enormous difficulty accepting praise, money, or other rewards, even when well deserved
Takes care of others without hesitation or being asked	Has great difficulty accepting help from others
Gets promoted often and rises within most organizations	Each promotion comes with a spasm of guilt, a feeling of "I don't deserve this," even though the promotion is well deserved
Brings success to the organization, while always giving credit to others	Feels pained and embarrassed in being feted or praised

People like Mary, who lose their focus due to altruism and an inborn, unstoppable sensitivity to others, make up a large segment of the population. We read every day about the opposite type, the talented narcissists who build empires but ruin the lives of people around them. When we do read about people like Mary, it's usually in a context of a human interest story or the pathological side of the coin, the codependent, or the enabler.

In this chapter, I've expanded the frame to show the strength people like Mary possess and the great good they can do. On the other hand, they often allow themselves to be taken advantage of. That's why toxic handlers need handlers, too. Mary needed counseling not only for the sake of her marriage, but for the sake of her career, her physical health, and her well-being. Mary needed something better than the Prozac that her doctor reflexively refilled. She needed to understand both the advantages and disadvantages that come with her uncanny ability to read people and to make them feel good.

Paradoxically, what saved her as a child led her to sabotage herself as an adult. We see it often: people behaving self-destructively in adulthood by enacting patterns that saved them in childhood. In addition to Mary, think of the child who retreated into a fantasy world to save herself back then, or the child who learned to lie artfully to avoid her father's sadistic attacks, or the child who learned too well how to please others to avoid danger, and how maladaptive those stratagems become in adulthood.

To help Mary learn how to focus on herself rather than sacrifice herself for the good of the group, I had to help her defuse a fairly common, elaborately wired time bomb. As a child, Mary could not allow herself to feel how angry she truly was. She could not afford to feel anger at her father because she believed if she did, she and the rest of her family would perish. So she developed the habit of acting in the opposite way of what her deepest, truest feelings would have her do.

My work with Mary took time. There is no quick fix for what Mary— or what the other five characters I discuss—wrestled with. We live now in an age of fast-food psychiatry, which is about as nourishing as any fast food. People have grown impatient with long-term psychotherapy, or long-term anything, lampooning them as "Woody Allen therapy," ineffective, never-ending, self-indulgent. Instead we rely on the most common psychiatric intervention by far: medication. Medication is fast-acting, painless, relatively inexpensive, and convenient. It often helps. As I have stated, I prescribe medication regularly. But, I also know it never does all that needs to be done.

We would do well to regain a respect for therapies that allow enough time for a person to change maladaptive patterns of behavior and, to use a turn of phrase that has gone out of fashion, to work things through. Since Mary's very survival, and that of her family, depended on her keeping her anger unconscious, it would require first of all the creation of a safe and trusting relationship with me before we could touch that anger. However, until we arrived at such a safe and trusting place, and indeed, while we were getting to such a place, I could and did coach her on ways to take care of herself, while also taking care of others. Most of all, I helped her discover that, as an adult, it was safe now to let other people take care of themselves. No longer did she have to do it all.

But all that took time. Like the other people in this book, she was desperate when I met her. That was good. The moments when we feel most lost, most near collapse, most vulnerable are the moments when, with the right help, and with a touch of luck or grace, we can do what might have been impossible before.

As William James observed some hundred years ago:

> Most people live, whether physically, intellectually, or morally, in a very restricted circle of their potential being. They *make use* of a very small portion of their possible consciousness, and of their soul's resources in general, much like a man who, out of his whole bodily organism, should get into a habit of using and moving only his little finger. Great emergencies and crises show us how much greater our vital resources are than we had supposed.[11]

Forcing a person to dig deep is the good result of a crisis. In a crisis, we are most apt to wake up, shiver, and change. Of course, it is also when we are most apt to ruin our lives. Whether the moment of crisis veers one way or the other depends upon how the individual deals not just with the facts of the situation but, more importantly, with the flames of emotion it creates. Put differently, the person bearing with the intensity of the emotions, rather than fleeing the scene or attacking some imagined enemy, determines the wisdom with which he or she can deal with the facts.

The key to bearing with the emotions is to reach out to someone else, to never worry alone, as my old teacher used to say. Worrying alone, *especially* in a crisis, leads to disaster. But, if you worry with the right person, the crisis can open you up and lay bare what's wrong. Intense emotion can rip a person apart, but, handled with skill, such emotion can serve as a scalpel that cuts opens the psyche in a way nothing else can and allow for surgical cure.

As José Ortega y Gasset wrote some eighty years ago:

> Take stock of those around you and you will see them wandering about lost through life, like sleep-walkers in the midst of their good or evil fortune, without the slightest suspicion of what is happening to them . . . Life is at the start a chaos in which one is lost. The individual suspects this but he is frightened at finding himself face to face with this terrible reality, and tries to cover it over with a curtain of fantasy, where everything is clear. It does not worry him that his "ideas" are not true, he uses them as trenches for the defense of his existence, as scarecrows to frighten away reality.
>
> The man with the clear head is the man who frees himself from these fantastic "ideas" and looks life in the face, realizes that everything in it is problematic, and feels himself lost. As this is the simple truth—that to live is to feel lost—he who accepts it has already begun to find himself, to be on firm ground. Instinctively, as do the shipwrecked, he will look round for something to which to cling,

and that tragic, ruthless glance, absolutely sincere because it is a question of his salvation, will cause him to bring order into the chaos of his life. These are the only genuine ideas; the ideas of the shipwrecked. All the rest is rhetoric, posturing, farce.[12]

In crises, we find our ideas of the shipwrecked. We cut through the haze and out of necessity find what we need. Which Mary did.

With Mary—and the many other people like Mary I've worked with—the greatest agent of change was the love that developed between the two of us. Love has become a dangerous word, sometimes for good reason. But, for better or worse, love remains the most powerful tool for good we have in this life. Love between a therapist and a client is unique in that the two people see each other only in an office, at set times for a set amount of time, and all they do there is talk. Furthermore, the focus is mainly on one person, the client. While the personality of the therapist certainly enters, the details of the therapist's life don't get much air time, nor should they.

What develops over time, when the process goes well, is a deep and abiding respect, care, and infusion of formative energy each person feels from the other. Call it love. It is a kind of love that has no exact duplicate elsewhere in life; perhaps the closest to it is the love that develops between a person and a certain composer's music, a certain artist's paintings, or a certain writer's novels.

It takes time for this love to reach a level where it can effect change. You get there through chitchat as well as the discussion of big topics and important events. The process still mystifies me, but I have personally seen it work so often, both as a client and as a therapist, that I know its power is real.

When I am the therapist, I don't wield the power. Nor does my client. We wield it together, week after week, session after session. I don't know any other way for a person like Mary to reach a place of freedom and positive self-regard than through a loving relationship. It does not have to be with a therapist, but that is one controlled way to do it. Most people who tend to take care of others first do not have the major childhood antecedents

Mary had, and so do not need to go into the depth she needed to. For those, I will offer some tips.

But first, as with Les, Jean, Ashley, and Jack, I note the dangers Mary created for herself, using the basic plan as an outline:

1. ENERGY. Taking care of others is mentally exhausting.

2. EMOTION. A strange mental exchange occurs when you take on other people's stuff, their negative emotions. It's called projective identification, which is a fancy term that means you, the handler, get filled with the toxic stuff that fills the person you're helping. You then launder the dirty clothes, so to speak, by holding them for a while, then returning the cleaned-up material to the person you're helping. All this puts you in a precarious state emotionally yourself.

3. ENGAGEMENT. Engaging with other people's problems curtails your ability to engage with your own work.

4. STRUCTURE. You tend to ignore the structures that would guide you to take care of yourself if you are taking care of others too much.

5. CONTROL. Your reflex to help others starts to control you if you don't understand what's happening and take steps to prevent it.

WHAT TO DO ABOUT IT

10 tips for helping you take care of yourself, not just everyone else

1 Recognize that your gut reaction—your reflexive, subconscious, emotional, initial response—is to take care of others first. Realize that your set point is to make sure everyone else in the organization is happy, before you tend to your own situation.

2 Recognize that this tendency is admirable in many ways and extremely valuable to the organization, *as long as you couple it with an ability to take care of yourself.*

3 Understand that taking care of yourself is not the same as being selfish. That's why the airlines tell you to put the oxygen mask on yourself first. The reason they give you this perfectly obvious bit of advice is that so many of us are like Mary, inclined to take care of others first.

4 Think this through. You've got to get your head around the fact that taking care of yourself is good for the entire organization. Doing the opposite runs deep in many people, particularly women. Talk it through with others, until you understand that it is good, right, and necessary to take care of yourself if you are going to be of any use to anyone else.

5 Schedule time for yourself into your day. For example, set aside uninterrupted time to work on difficult problems; time to exercise or do yoga; time to get enough sleep; time for meditation, prayer, or some other reflective practice; and time for love making (yes, this is good for you).

6 Learn to say, "Let me think about that," rather than automatically saying yes. If you reset your automatic response to "Let me think about that," you will give yourself enough time to decide if it makes sense for you to take something on or if you can politely decline.

7 When someone you work with is in distress, consider if you are the best person to jump in and help. Once you've jumped in, it's hard to jump out. So jump in only if (a) you have time to take on what could be a prolonged project; (b) if you are the person best qualified to provide the help needed; and (c) you have the energy and emotional reserves to offer the help needed.

8 Learn to ask for help. Most caretakers are what's called "counter-dependent," which means they are far more comfortable providing help than receiving it. Go outside your comfort zone and learn to ask for help. People will feel pleased that you asked. As you know only too well, it feels good to be needed.

9 Remember, if you don't have the time or energy to provide help, someone else in the organization can help. And the less you help, the more others will fill the void you create.

10 Finally, for all your efforts, be glad of who you are. As problems go, being a caretaker is a good one to have. The world benefits from you a lot. You've just got to learn to pull back a bit so you can survive and thrive.

dropping the ball

how to stop underachieving at work

"I hate myself!" Sharon said to the wall. Sitting at her desk, she had just realized that she'd spaced out on a conference call she was supposed to have been on for the past hour. She'd thought the call was to take place tomorrow, until she'd looked down at her planner and saw that it was scheduled for today.

Her mind raced. *Why didn't I check my planner when I got to the office? Why do I resolve to do it every day, then not do it? Why do I know what I'm supposed to do, but then not do what I'm supposed to do? Do I have some kind of a fear of failure? Do I secretly want to ruin my life? Am I trying to fail in order to please my mother, or am I afraid of surpassing her? Why hasn't all the f–ing therapy I've had not done a damn thing to help me? Is there any hope? Am I doomed to live this pattern out over and over and over again? Why doesn't someone just shoot me?*

Avery, one of her colleagues at the magazine, who was also a friend, walked by her office and could see Sharon was in distress. "What's wrong, hon?" Avery asked.

Sharon sighed. "You don't want to hear. I'm a loser, that's the long and short of it. I just missed the conference call with Tony's group, and I'm sure that will be the last straw for them. What could have been a golden opportunity turns into another swing and miss by good old Sharon. I am so over being me."

"Sharon, hon, you're the most talented person at this magazine. I wish I had half your ability."

"I love you, Avery, but do you know how tired I am of hearing how much potential I have? What's the good of having potential if you can never live up to it? I wish I'd been born dumb as a post. Then I wouldn't have to live up to anything, which I can't do anyway."

"You know what," Avery replied, "I've gotta go take care of a couple of things right now, but I am coming back here at five sharp and I am taking you across the street to the Algonquin for a couple of the best mojitos you've ever had. And you are not allowed to say no!"

"Thanks, Avery. Gives me something to look forward to."

———————

Unlike the previous five examples, Sharon's story is not about ADT, but rather true attention deficit hyperactivity disorder (ADHD). I include it because ADHD is far more common in adults than most people realize, affecting at least five million adults in the United States, 80 percent of whom are not diagnosed. Treating ADHD in an adult can change that person's life dramatically for the better.

Thirty-nine-year-old Sharon had worked as a senior editor at a major women's magazine for years. She'd risen through the ranks, but she had been unable to reach the top tier due to a chronic problem with planning, prioritizing, and following through. In fact, had it not been for her considerable talent and brilliance, she would have been let go long ago.

People who have ADHD tend to agree with the following statements.

Planning is very difficult for me.

Procrastination is my middle name.

I love crises; that's when I focus best.

I am long on imagination but short on follow-through.

I'd rather have a root canal than attend a meeting.

I am frustrated because I am not making the best use of my talents.

I'm impulsive.

Punctuality is a problem for me.

I get irritated with people who are not as mentally quick as I am.

I do things whole hog, even to excess.

Sharon made sense, albeit an intensely painful sense, of her under-achieving ways by chastising herself in an unremittingly harsh inner voice. She reserved her sharpest condemnations in life not for anyone or anything else but for herself, routinely invoking coarse terms like loser, slacker, airhead, ditz, fraud, cheat, charlatan, idiot, pathetic, or weak. As inaccurate as all those terms were—and the sane part of her knew they were wildly inaccurate—she felt better, for some weird reason, lacerating her mind and soul than living without knowing why she'd never been able to make the most of her immense talents.

Author Byron Katie, in her musings on how we hold ourselves back in life, suggests asking yourself the liberating question, "Who would you be without that thought?" But Sharon couldn't imagine being without that thought, in her case, her many thoughts of how inept and inadequate she was. She made a moral diagnosis of herself and clung to it. She felt she'd be crippled without self-condemnation. She was unable to let go of the thoughts that did her in, in her own mind, because without them she would be left with no explanation at all. It was as if her self-condemnation provided a skeleton upon which the rest of her could hang.

Right now, as Avery had discovered, she was in a deep funk. Every once in a while, it hit her hard: how much she'd underachieved in her life, how everyone in high school and college had thought she'd become an important novelist, only to see that dream yield to her need to make a living. Hence, the compromise of editorial work.

In this funk, she found it impossible to focus on the work she had to do. Her feelings of shame and dismay shot through her like a singeing current, carrying pain throughout her body and soul. But she was also tough as sinew. Like a kicked mutt who knows how to survive, she knew how to fight through anything. Fight. That had been her chief coping style her whole life. She spoke no words to herself when she had to act; she just took action. Deeper than words, a titanic storm of determination roiled within her that would never allow her to give up. So through the funk, she fought.

Sharon's backstory

Twelve weeks premature at birth, Sharon had had to fight from the moment she entered the world. Her dad, Douglas, doted on her, but her mom competed with her. She learned from her mother, and her three older brothers, that she had to fight to survive. "It's your red hair," her dad would say. "It's why you're such a pistol."

Sharon was both the daughter her dad had always wanted and the daughter her mother had never wanted. Elaine, Sharon's mom, herself had grown up under the critical eye of an exacting, cold mother. Elaine had been able to develop affection for her boys, but she'd always sensed that a daughter would only bring out the worst in her, just as she'd brought out the worst in her own mother.

And how right she turned out to be. Elaine competed with baby Sharon for Douglas's attention. When Douglas doted on Sharon, Elaine would either fly into a rage or sulk, or both. Fortunately, Douglas wouldn't let his wife separate him from his daughter, so their relationship flourished. But Elaine tried to undermine Sharon every step of the way. It was as if her worst nightmare was that her daughter would succeed and find the joy in childhood she herself had never found.

Whether it was her red hair, as her dad said, or a fighter's genes, Sharon needed every bit of extra energy she could summon not only to fend off her mother but to get an education and do it right. Her parents had high expectations for the four kids, but their expectations were nothing compared to Sharon's expectations for herself. She wanted to win at everything, excel at everything, and be number one, no matter what the activity or task.

Schoolwork did not come easily. Not only did Sharon have her mother's constant undermining criticisms to deal with, but her mind also wandered all the time. She would be looking out the window when the teacher called on her, and she'd be publicly embarrassed by her inability to respond. Rather than give up, though, she bore down. She borrowed notes, she went for extra help, she stayed in and studied while others played, and she saw to it that she did excel. She got A's. If she ever got a B, God help that teacher, because Sharon would be back in, not to argue for a higher grade, but to get extra help every day.

She also took to sports with abandon. She ran track and found exhilaration in running. In winter, she found the same high in swimming. She wanted to dive, too, but since she could not do both for the team, she chose to swim, just to prove that she could endure the physical punishment that long-distance swimming demanded. Pain turned into pleasure when she reached a certain point in her workouts. She thanked her mother for this: she courted extreme sports and high achievement to win the battle her mother had drawn her into.

Then, in tenth grade, an English teacher, Mr. Elliot, changed her life. He turned Sharon on to literature, starting with the poetry of Emily Dickinson. Sharon loved the brief lines, the short takes. "I heard a fly buzz when I died . . . " Lines like that amazed and delighted Sharon in a way nothing in school had before. Lines from Dickinson's poem about a snake embedded in Sharon's mind: "But never met this fellow, Attended or alone / Without a tighter breathing, And zero at the bone." Zero at the bone? How perfect, she thought, how exactly perfect. But how did she think of that phrase, "zero at the bone." Where did it come from? She wanted desperately to know, so she could make such lines come to her as well.

With Mr. Elliot's encouragement, Sharon set to find out where such surprises actually do come from. "They come from your unconscious, your imagination," Mr. Elliot had said. "You have a great imagination. Try trusting it."

"What do you mean?" Sharon had asked.

"You are so tenacious. That's great, but sometimes you just need to let go of control and let your mind surprise you. I can guarantee you, Emily Dickinson was as surprised as anyone when she wrote the words, 'zero at the bone.'"

From then on, Sharon had found a new playground, her favorite playground, the world of imagination, images, and words. She wrote poetry in the manner of Dickinson, but gradually it grew into the manner of Sharon. She also wrote prose and was a natural storyteller. Over time, from tenth grade on, she found her own voice so that she could write without faking it or imitating someone else. She looked forward to college and the delights she knew she'd take in literature.

But, due to her problems with sustaining focus on tests, she scored poorly on the SATs and did not get into the Ivy League colleges she'd hoped to attend. Due to her excellent grades and recommendations, however, she did get into a number of good colleges. She ended up choosing Hobart and William Smith Colleges in upstate New York. She embraced literature and writing there. However, she found that she could not sustain a story long enough to turn it into something substantial. She became editor of the college literary magazine, but she did not publish much of her own writing.

Her mother carped, "Be more practical. We won't support you, and there's no money in being a failed writer." Sharon knew that her mother would cringe in envy if she succeeded as a writer, but she did see that her mother had a point. The last thing she wanted to do was give her mother the satisfaction of seeing Sharon beg for financial help. She did have to make a living, so after school she entered a world she knew she could excel in, the world of editing.

Her dreams fading, she nonetheless did well in her career. All her supervisors recognized what Mr. Elliot had seen: great talent, drive, and imagination. She knew she was different from other people, though, in a way she could not explain, nor could others understand. When a friend or colleague would say, "Sharon, you're so talented. Why don't you get an organizer or a coach or something so you can make the most of what you've got?" she didn't know how to explain that she just couldn't. Out of sheer frustration, out of the need for an answer—any answer—she began to invoke the black list of hateful terms she applied to herself, like daily punishments.

When one of her brothers would ask, "Why can't you last in a relationship with a guy? Aren't any of them good enough for you?" she didn't know how to explain that it was she who felt inadequate and not up to the task of connecting in a normal way. So she'd say, "I'm just a selfish person." As wrong as that was, it was an answer.

She also detected many correct answers, not about herself, but about others and the world. She had a knack—both a gift and a curse—for seeing what other people did not see. She could see into a person in a second, tell a phony in a heartbeat, and know what someone else was thinking simply by looking at them or diagnosing what was really going on in a meeting in seconds. (The word "diagnosis" literally means "knowing through.") Sharon could know through anyone and anything; it was as if she had X-ray vision. This perceptiveness could help her but, often as not, it could also isolate her, because she could not easily share what she knew. She carried with her so much emotion, so much insight, that it could wear her out.

She tried to use her editing as a way of getting down to the concrete and practical, so as to avoid the thoughts and feelings that always pulsed through her. But even in editing, she could tell a false voice on the page; she could see a manipulative writer work his way from sentence to sentence, and, at times, it was all she could do not to scream in frustration at reading the stuff. She'd grip her desk, in an effort to control her mind. But try as she might, her mental focus resembled a toddler on a picnic. It went wherever it wanted to go, with no regard for danger or authority. Controlling it was beyond difficult. It felt impossible.

She knew, deep inside, that if she could only find the key to sustaining her focus, she could write the novels and the stories she had in her, and she could sustain a relationship with a man. She could fulfill another dream, become a mother, and be the kind of mother she wished she'd had herself.

But for now, all of that eluded her, and she felt ashamed. She'd never give in, she knew this as she sat at her desk, but she wondered what would become of her.

life with ADHD

One of the millions of adults in the United States who have undiagnosed attention deficit hyperactivity disorder, Sharon had a chance to change her life for the better in a big way. There is no diagnosis relating to the mind that carries with it a more dramatic opportunity for changing a life for the better, and yet, as I've stated, at least 80 percent of adults who have ADHD don't know it. So they languish, and they underachieve, like Sharon. Some get into severe trouble. The prisons are full of adults with undiagnosed ADHD, as are the lines of the unemployed, the drug and alcohol addicted, the accident-prone, the depressed and anxious, and the marginalized.

Fortunately, due to her tenacity and native talent, Sharon had done well, compared to the millions whom ADHD severely impairs. But she still was underachieving in a major way, and she knew it. It was a matter of time before depression and even despair took her down further, to a point she would be unable to do what she was doing.

For various reasons, most people, including most doctors, do not know much, if anything about ADHD in adults. They believe it is a childhood condition of overactive boys. As a result, the millions of adults who could become hugely successful once their ADHD is treated never get the help they so desperately need. With proper help, adults who have this trait can excel at the highest level. Nobel Prize winners, Pulitzer Prize winners, self-made billionaires, Academy Award winners, entrepreneurs of all kinds, and various others at the top of their fields all share this fascinating, widely misunderstood trait.

What makes ADHD so interesting is that it is composed of such beneficial and problematic elements (see table 6-1). Treatment aims to take advantage of the positives, while limiting the damage done by the negatives.

I've been working with adults who have ADHD since I first learned about it in 1981. I have the condition myself, as well as dyslexia. I've learned that with proper management, these conditions can actually be turned into prime assets in one's life. That's why I see myself not as a specialist in treating disabilities, but as a specialist in helping people unwrap their gifts.

TABLE 6-1

Beneficial and problematic characteristics of people with ADHD

Beneficial	Problematic
Creative	Goes off on tangents
Intuitive	Has difficulty citing evidence
Can hyper-focus when interested	Easily distracted when not interested
Passionate about work when interested	Can lose track of deadlines, procrastinate, show up late
Quick to act, does not waste time	Can be impulsive, make reckless decisions
Always searching for new, novel sources of stimulation	Searching for high stimulation can lead to trouble, such as dangerous behaviors or drug abuse
Energetic	Sometimes can't sit still and listen
Easily inspired and inspiring	Difficulty finishing projects or maintaining long-term relationships

With the proper diagnosis, Sharon could begin to unwrap her own gifts and undo the decades of disappointment and self-attack she's endured. Sharon, and the millions of adults like her, lives one insight away from embarking on new and improved life. People who have ADHD sabotage themselves, not due to some unconscious conflict, but because of the way that their brains are wired. They become victims of their brain's shortcomings, and cannot gain access to the brilliance their brain usually does possess.

Beyond just those who have ADHD, millions more underachieve because they don't know how to manage the brain they have. Some years ago, I wrote a children's story called "A Walk in the Rain with a Brain," which contains the refrain, "No brain is the same, no brain is the best, each brain finds its own special way." Due to the widespread failure of the educational system, as well as a paucity of experts on the subject of practical brain management, most people never come to understand and master their own brain's special way. They may not flounder, but neither do they excel as they otherwise could.

My first step in helping Sharon was to reframe her condition. She was stuck in a thicket from which she needed to be freed. Possessing great talent, she underachieved not through lack of effort or discipline, but because she suffered from untreated ADHD. Telling her to try harder would be like telling a person who is nearsighted to squint harder.

Our work together began with education. I recommended that she read my book, *Delivered from Distraction*, as it provides a quick way of learning a lot about ADHD. A fast reader, she was happy to do this, but were she not an avid reader, I would have asked her just to read the first chapter of the book, which is called, "The Skinny: Read This If You Can't Read the Whole Book." Once she understood ADHD and the positive qualities inherent in it—like creativity, spunk, originality, grit, and energy—then we started unwrapping.

Stimulant medications, like Ritalin or Adderall, can be a godsend. They work about 80 percent of the time. Medication for ADHD can be like eyeglasses. It helps a person focus more effectively. Used properly, it has no side effects other than appetite suppression without unwanted weight loss. Any other side effects can be eliminated by changing the dose or discontinuing the medication. (For more on the medications used to treat ADHD, see the appendix at the end of this book.) In addition to medication, the rest of the treatment includes exercise, nutrition, meditation, positive human contact, learning to get into the right place emotionally, and learning structure, which an ADHD coach can help with.

Coaching is a relatively new field. Many people represent themselves as ADHD coaches, but, since the field is not regulated, it can be difficult to find a qualified coach worth the time and money you invest. I recommend three groups whose personnel I can vouch for: ADD Coach Academy (addca.com), ADHD Coaches Organization (adhdcoaches.org), and the Edge Foundation (edgefoundation.org).

As with all adults who have undiagnosed ADHD, Sharon simply didn't know that a treatable condition was holding her back. It was as if she were driving on square wheels. The shipwreck of her life was that she had given up her dreams, dreams that she actually could achieve. Luckily, the stimulant, Adderall, helped Sharon immediately. With an 80 percent track record, *lucky* is perhaps the wrong word. In any case, as so often happens, Sharon got immediate benefit from medication.

She then became able to rethink all that had happened to her until the time we met. A born fighter, she got angry that this diagnosis had been missed, but that anger only fueled her desire to reach for the dreams she'd never quite forgotten. The easy part of the treatment was taking the medication. It helped her focus quite dramatically. It turned her square wheels into round ones. But this was only the beginning. She had lived her entire life with a negative view of herself. As spunky, driven, and resilient as she was, she suffered inside.

The damage done early in life to those who have learning differences can be traumatic. One of my friends, David Neeleman, is the founder of JetBlue Airways. Neeleman has ADHD in spades. The day JetBlue went public, Neeleman made millions of dollars in a matter of hours. He told me, "Driving home that night, was I looking forward to celebrating? No, I felt like the same loser who couldn't hack it in high school."

We don't have a medication to revamp a person's self-image. With Sharon, I did what I do with all the adults I diagnose and treat. I sat with her, listened, explored, bore the pain with her, and gradually detoxified many of conflicted feelings that came up. She was excited to have a new life, to have round wheels. But she was also confused and angry. Why had it taken so long to find out? Why had no one picked up on it when she was in school? And why had her mother been so critical, rather than helpful?

Addressing all this takes time. Gradually, though, Sharon reawakened her dreams of writing and her faith in her own ability, and she started writing regularly. It's never too late. My oldest patient is eighty-six. He came to see me because he'd been trying to write a book his entire life. Once we diagnosed and treated his ADHD, he was able to begin the book.

Here's how the basic plan applied to Sharon's ADHD:

1. ENERGY. Sharon had a ton of energy, as most people with ADHD do, but she was not able to direct it or control it.

2. EMOTION. Her emotions fluctuated so much that it was difficult for her to stay in a steady emotional state.

3. ENGAGEMENT. Sharon's focus came and went. At times she could reach a state of acute focus and engage, at other times not at all.

4. STRUCTURE. Sharon had great difficulty in creating the basic structures—lists, plans, schedules—that are essential for success.

5. CONTROL. Sharon has great difficulty controlling the power of her mind. It was like a Ferrari with no brakes.

WHAT TO DO ABOUT IT
10 tips for adults who have ADHD

1. Learn as much as you can about the condition. Misconceptions and wrong information about ADHD are prevalent on the internet, so don't start there. Read my book *Delivered from Distraction* (coauthored with John Ratey), or *Fast Minds: How to Thrive If You Have Adult ADHD* by Craig Surman, MD, Tim Bilkey, and Karen Weintraub; *Taking Charge of Adult ADHD* by Russell Barkley, PhD; or *The Mindfulness Prescription for Adult ADHD* by Lidia Zylowska, MD, and Daniel Siegel.

2. Embrace ADHD, even though the term is terrible. ADHD does not involve a deficit of attention, but rather wandering. Hyperactivity is

usually absent in adults. And it is not a disorder, in my opinion, but rather a trait, which can serve a person wonderfully well as long as she manages it properly. The analogy I use with children applies to adults just as well: I tell them they have a Ferrari engine for a brain, with bicycle brakes. A Ferrari with no brakes is dangerous, but once the brakes get strengthened, then they're champions in the making. And, as I tell the kids, I am a brake specialist.

3 Understand that it is ADHD, and not some moral failing or deficiency in character, that has held you back and caused chronic underachievement. With proper management, the sky is now the limit.

4 Work with a doctor who has experience in helping adults with ADHD and who endorses a strength-based approach. Finding such a person may take some legwork, but it is worth putting in the effort. You might start with the department of psychiatry at the medical school nearest you.

5 Be proud of what you've got, because the positives can't be bought and can't be taught, while the negatives can be dealt with, once you find the right help. I've renamed this trait "the American Edge," as our gene pool is full of it. Just think of who came to this country in the waves of immigration and colonized it: dreamers, explorers, pioneers, risk takers, innovators, and entrepreneurs. Indeed, most entrepreneurs have ADHD.

6 Work with a coach to help develop skills of organization and time management. You might also download an app I created called CrazyBusy. It helps you prioritize tasks, assess the value of a given task, and organize tasks; it gives various tips, has a timer and stopwatch, offers guided meditation, and contains various tips on dealing with fast-paced life.

7   Meditation, physical exercise, proper nutrition, and sufficient sleep all make ADHD—and life in general—better.

8   Don't fear medication. Used properly, it can be as helpful as eyeglasses. Just make sure you work with a qualified doctor.

9   Do what you're good at as much as possible. Many adults with ADHD feel compelled to try to get good at what they're bad at, and waste a lot of time in the process.

10 Share what you've learned with others. ADHD in adults remains vastly unrecognized. Once you reap the benefits of diagnosis and treatment, share that with others to whom it might apply.

training your attention

how to manage and maintain
your ability to focus

flexible focus

creating the optimal state for excellence

In March 2012, Bubba Watson, a professional golfer, held a three-shot lead over the competition heading into Sunday's final round in the Doral Open at the Blue Monster course in Doral, Florida. For a pro golfer, a three-shot lead in the final round is by no means safe, but it is solid. Bubba was an odds-on favorite to win the tournament when he teed off Sunday.

One of the longest hitters in the game and, by most accounts, its most creative inventor of shots on the spot, Watson had all the talent in the world. What he lacked was focus. At Doral, he faltered on the front nine holes and lost his three-stroke lead. The tournament suddenly became a tense race to the finish. On television, commentator Johnny Miller criticized Watson for his inability to stay focused, lamenting that if he could ever learn how to focus consistently, he'd win many championships. Experts all agreed that Watson's lack of sustained focus held him back from achieving greatness.

However, something changed in Watson when he played later that year at the Masters Golf Tournament at Augusta National in Georgia. On one of the greatest stages in all of golf, at the tournament and course created by golf's greatest folk hero, Bobby Jones, Watson discovered his elusive focus.

Going into Sunday's final round of the Masters, he trailed the leader of the tournament by two shots. He was within striking distance, for sure. But on the fourth hole, something happened that would normally have knocked Watson off his game and into a tailspin. His competitor, Louis Oosthuizen, made one of the most spectacular shots in golf history. He made what's called a "double eagle." (If you're not familiar with the game, an "eagle" is a score two below par on a given hole—"par" being the score a player would get if he played each shot properly on a given hole. One under par on a hole is excellent; it is called a "birdie." Two under par is extraordinary; it is called an eagle. Three under par on one hole is almost unheard of; it is called a double eagle.) Oosthuizen scored an otherworldly two on the par-five fourth hole, one of the most amazing scores ever put up in golf history during one of its most storied tournaments.

If there were ever a time for Watson to lose his focus, playing along with Oosthuizen when he made the double eagle would have been it. But after seeing his competitor make golf history, Watson didn't blow up or choke. Instead, he bore down. He gained focus, rather than losing it, and avoided the disasters that had plagued him in the past.

By the eighteenth hole, both Watson and Oosthuizen were in position to win the tournament, provided either of them could sink just one putt on the eighteenth green. But both of them missed. The tournament headed into a "sudden death" playoff. In golf, nothing is tenser than sudden death; it means that the first player to win a hole wins the tournament; the other player goes home.

On the first hole of the sudden-death playoff, both players once again had a chance to win, but failed to make their putts. The tournament headed into a second hole of sudden death. This time around, Watson made an errant swing, driving his ball far to the right and into the tall pine trees that border the fairway (the landing area a player aims for when he hits his drive). It looked like disaster, a sure defeat. It seemed that his old demon, lack of focus, had finally bitten him and taken him down. He had hit a really bad shot, and at the worst possible time. "Bubba Blows It"—that would be the headline Monday morning and on tweets in the minutes to come.

But it didn't work out that way. Watson found his ball some thirty yards deep into the woods, sitting embarrassedly on a bed of pine straw. The logical play, the play every sensible golfer would make, would be to hit a safe shot from the trees out onto the fairway, try to make par, and hope Oosthuizen didn't make birdie. There was no other realistic shot, besides the safe shot out onto the fairway. Or so it seemed to everyone in the world who was watching.

Except to Watson. He'd say later that he'd been at the same place in the woods before, so the choice of shot was a no-brainer. Wasting little time, he took his stance and, using a special grip and swing of his own invention, hit his ball out from under the overhanging trees.

He had to make his ball do the seemingly impossible. The ball had to go straight and up to escape the overhanging trees, and then it had to make a right turn. Expert players can make a ball go straight, or they can make it turn right, but to do both on the same shot requires extraordinary skill or, some would say, magical powers.

Watson made his ball perform that magic. It flew up and away, obediently taking a sharp right at just the right juncture, curving some forty yards, and then it floated down onto the green where it rolled to within fifteen feet of the cup. Now Oosthuizen didn't stand a chance. Watson won the tournament, to everyone's total amazement.

What happened to Watson at the Masters? No one knows just how he did it. Most people agreed that he looked different than he usually did. His jaw was set, his eyes looked straight ahead, he didn't goof around with the gallery, and he displayed none of his usual outward signs of distraction.

Some thought it had something to do with the fact that he and his wife had adopted their first child just days before the tournament. When Watson went off to Augusta, his wife and baby had to stay home because the infant was too young to travel. But in his mind, they were right there with him. (As both a parent and a child psychiatrist, I believe that nothing changes a person more dramatically and permanently than the experience of becoming a parent. At that moment a person enters into a permanent state of psychosis. You fall insanely in love with the squirming, squalling, peeing-and-pooping machine you've just brought into the world.)

Where Watson found his focus is anybody's guess. But that he found it is beyond question. My guess is that he took advantage of three factors that, in combination, create mental focus. They are structure, novelty, and motivation. Every golf shot combines all three. The game is highly structured. Each shot is unique in its own way, hence, novel. And the player wants to do well, hence, the motivation.

I believe Oosthuizen's double eagle on the fourth hole served to get Watson's attention and motivate him. For a moment, on the second hole of sudden death, Watson relapsed, lost focus, and hit a ball into the trees. But then, faced with an impossible shot, he drew on his creativity and hit the shot of his life.

what is flexible focus?

Focus varies in its intensity and duration. At one extreme is the absence of focus (without being asleep, drunk, in a coma, or deprived of focus by some other physical cause). I call this aimless, meandering state "drift." It can be a sweet state, indeed, or a time waster. Your mind simply drifts along, like a fisherman trawling. Sometimes, in drift, you catch a big fish.

You don't know it, but your brain uses these seemingly empty moments to do a lot of work. It goes into what's called "default mode," activating the default network, or DN. Particularly active in these moments of daydreaming or drift are the lateral prefrontal cortex and the dorsal anterior cingulate cortex, both of which are crucial in so-called executive function, which includes planning and focusing attention.

This explains, in part, why you need to look away from what you're doing from time to time, to drift, to take a break mentally. Your brain does not take a break during these periods. Quite the opposite. It stokes up on energy, element number one in the basic plan, equipping you for the next period of paying close attention.

You might think the brain would consume more energy when working on a problem or concentrating on a task, but it doesn't. When in drift, the DN consumes just as much, if not more, energy than when deeply in focus mode. Interestingly, in drift or in DN, what you think about (since your brain never goes empty) is usually other people, yourself, and the relationships among those. You engage in "social cognition." Nature wired us to think socially during its down times. As psychologist Matthew Lieberman, a pioneer in social neuroscience, put it, "There are so many other things our brain could have been wired to spend its spare time on—learning calculus, improving our logical reasoning ability, cataloging variations in the classes of objects we have seen. Any of these could have adaptive value. But nature placed its bet on our thinking socially."[1]

At the other extreme of drift is "flow." The psychologist who researched this heightened state of awareness, Mihaly Csikszentmihalyi, named this most focused state of mind in 1975.[2] In flow, a person becomes so immersed in what he is doing that he loses self-consciousness altogether. He gets so into what he is doing that he merges with the action he is involved in, becoming one with it. He loses his sense of time, even his awareness of his biological needs and drives, a state reminiscent of William Butler Yeats's lines: "O body swayed to music, O brightening glance, / How can we know the dancer from the dance?"[3]

Like all moments of peak intensity, flow fades. Almost all of us have entered into flow at one time or another, so we know firsthand that it doesn't last. Some people find flow while running or doing yoga; others while playing music, meditating, knitting, doing crossword puzzles; others while risking their lives skiing downhill or sweating over a piece of sculpture.

According to Csikszentmihalyi's research, corroborated by many people I've interviewed as well as my own experience, in flow a person experiences life at its peak, its most joyful, its most intensely fulfilling. It is also the state in which people exceed their personal best, often achieving much better work than they've ever done before. So absorbing, however, is the flow state that you only recollect the high of it, the pure joy of it. Since you lose self-consciousness when you're in flow, you're not aware of how great it is until it's over.

But you can't spend your whole day in flow. You need to eat and sleep. Furthermore, the brain in that state is limited by its supply of neurotransmitters. With practice, however, you can learn to enter flow regularly. The key is to engage in some activity that both matters to you deeply and is challenging, so that you have to stretch.

Csikszentmihalyi's work has been extended in practical directions by Steven Kotler, director of research for the Flow Genome Project, an international, transdisciplinary organization dedicated to decoding what happens during flow.[4] Kotler and his group are developing methods for "hacking flow," as he puts it, as it occurs in everyday life.[5] Most of his research has been with athletes who do extreme sports that often put their lives in danger. He's found that these athletes access flow regularly and that when they do, they routinely exceed their personal best. In these cases, great gain comes with great risk.

But it is a safe assumption that most people do not want to put their lives in danger in order to access flow. For us—and I certainly include myself in this group—the doorway to flow still remains open. We need to select those activities that both challenge us and matter deeply to us.

For example, in my case, this challenge comes with writing. I have a love-hate relationship with writing; most writers do. That's because writing is beyond challenging; at times, it seems impossible. The writing is almost never as good as it could be or as the writer hopes it will be, so the task promises disappointment at every turn. That's why we writers often avoid writing. When Ernest Hemingway was asked how to write a novel, he replied, "The first thing you do is clean out the refrigerator." He meant that writers will do just about anything to avoid putting words onto a page.

Yet, we love what we do too. Few things please me more than creating a well-turned sentence or describing an image that does its job succinctly. (I hope you find a few in this book.) They are my reasons for coming back to the blank page, just as the great shot is the golfer's reason for coming back to the tee, in spite of all his bad shots. When I finally do sit down at the keyboard, I typically enter flow—usually for minutes, but sometimes for an hour. The difference between my experience with writing and that of, say, the extreme skier is that I do not have the element of danger to keep me riveted in flow for extended periods. As a result, flow comes and goes as I write. (I suppose if I were writing with my life on the line, I might remain in flow for a longer time.)

Short of flow, there is focus. We all know what focus is. It is the standard term for a concentrated, clear state of mind, focused on one target. Between focus and flow lies what I call "flexible focus." It differs from flow in that it's not the high that flow is; it's a way of tapping into some of the qualities of flow without being so absorbed that you can't attend to anything else. In a state of flexible focus, you retain the ability to concentrate on a task, while at the same time remaining open to new input.

Flexible focus is a hybrid of flow that's accessible in everyday life. When in a state of flexible focus, you have a semipermeable boundary around your mind that allows for some distraction and sometimes the arrival of a new and important idea.

For example, consider the case of David Neeleman, the founder of Jet-Blue. Neeleman invented the electronic ticket, one of the most important innovations in the business of aviation in the past twenty years. "I didn't plan to do it," he told me. "I just saw the idea one day. It seemed so obvious. I didn't understand why someone else hadn't already thought of it. But, in fact, everyone else in the business laughed at me, saying, 'No one will go to the airport without a paper ticket.' Of course, now we all do, and it's saved the industry many millions and saved customers all kinds of anxiety and missed flights."

"What led to the idea?" I asked.

"Nothing," Neeleman said. "Other than that I'm always thinking of ways to improve the business. That's really all I do. Come up with ideas and develop them. The electronic ticket was just one of my better ones. But the process is the same with all of them. I get into a certain mode and ideas come."

Neeleman is not an artist; he's a businessman. But in thinking up the electronic ticket, his mind was in a state of open-minded readiness. He was pondering ways to improve efficiency, as most executives do. But instead of forcing an idea up from a rigid, established, well-trodden place—say, overvaluing or being invested in his own past experience or reading everything he could about improving efficiency—he put himself into a state of flexible focus, and the idea appeared.

Flexible focus embodies a paradox. In flexible focus, you hold on to and balance both the logical and creative parts of your brain at the same time. You combine both your creative powers with your powers to organize and analyze. You're able to take in new input without becoming sidetracked by it. You're able to stay on task but not rigidly so.

To achieve flexible focus, you instinctively balance right brain with left brain, creativity with discipline, randomness with organization. You can be searching while sticking with what you're doing, combining flexibility with rigor, spontaneity with structure, rule breaking with rule adherence. You can mix a new way with a proven way, and a journey with a goal. This is the great cerebral balancing act, the major skill, that allows you to master the challenges of your work and to take advantage of the opportunities with which modern life abounds. In achieving such a balance, you

ACHIEVE FOCUS THREE WORDS AT A TIME

1. **Turn it off (TIO).** Turn off your electronic devices during periods of the day when you want uninterrupted, focused time.

2. **Trust your way.** Perhaps the single-most clichéd song lyric ever, "I did it my way" became so clichéd because its message is so powerful. We focus best and do our best when we do it our way. We all have our routines, our own individualized process or way for producing our best work. Trust yours. When you don't know where you're headed, your process or way will allow your unconscious to enter. It will guide and often surprise you with your most valuable discoveries and unexpected solutions. Don't work against your grain, but with it.

3. **Take a break.** When you start to glaze over or feel frantic, stop what you are doing. Stand up, walk around, get a glass of water, stretch. Just sixty seconds can do the trick.

4. **Do something difficult.** People focus most intently when they take on a challenge, when they are working in an area where they are skilled, but where they are also stretched. Often, amazingly enough, what seemed impossible becomes possible.

5. **Ask for help.** Don't feel it is a sign of weakness to ask for help when you hit a snag. It's just the opposite, a sign of strength that can get you out of a confused place and back on track.

6. **Take your time.** One of the truest rules of modern life is if you don't take your time, someone or something else will take it from you. Guard your time jealously. It is your most prized possession. Do not give it away easily or let someone regulate it for you, unless you absolutely have to do so.

7. **Close your eyes.** When you are losing focus or feeling confused, the simple act of sitting back in your chair and closing your eyes can, oddly enough, allow you to see clearly. It can restore focus and provide a new direction.

8. **Draw a picture.** Visuals clarify thinking. Draw a diagram, construct a table, cover a page with zigzags like a child finger painting, cover a page with phrases and arrows, use colored pencils or markers. Draw on poster paper on an easel or on the floor, just get past words and blow up the frame to accommodate visuals of all kinds. You may soon see the bigger picture you'd been looking for coming into focus.

9. **Talk to yourself.** Talking aloud to yourself can lead you out of confusion. Assuming you are in a setting that allows for this, simply talk about the issue you are grappling with. Talking out loud engages a different part of the brain than thinking in silence. It can clear out the fog.

10. **Do what works.** Don't worry about convention or what's supposed to work. Some people focus better with music playing or in a noisy room. Some people focus better when walking or even running. Some people focus best in early morning, others late at night; some in cold rooms, others in a sauna; some while fasting, others while eating. There is no right way, *only the best way for you. Experiment and discover what works for you.*

gain access to unbidden, unexpected thoughts, images, impulses, and emotions that can deepen any mental activity, while you retain the ability to organize and develop the ideas you already have.

In their book *The Innovator's DNA*, Jeff Dyer, Hal Gregersen, and Clayton Christensen describe several of the characteristics common to innovative executives like Amazon's Jeff Bezos, Intuit's Scott Cook, and Salesforce.com's Marc Benioff.[6] Innovators like these tend to push boundaries and take the opposite position of established processes or ways of thinking. They free associate; they connect wildly different ideas, inputs, and disciplines. They observe things closely and gather ideas from everyday phenomena. They like to experiment. And they enjoy stretching their minds and experience through travel and meeting people from other walks of life. In short, they are open-minded, curious, and more likely to find their own way rather than follow a preset path.

In a Robert Frost poem quoted so often it has become cliché, the entire final stanza, with its memorable metric at the end, is worth reading:

I shall be telling this with a sigh
Somewhere ages and ages hence:
Two roads diverged in a wood, and I,
I took the one less traveled by,
And that has made all the difference.[7]

Novelty, the less traveled road, increases the chance for flexible focus, while repetition, conformity, and routine reduce that chance. However, too much novelty leads to chaos and confusion, which is why we need structure to bring novelty (and its generator, imagination) under control.

Let me illustrate flexible focus with another story of a recent breakthrough. Not only does the story illustrate flexible focus, but the discovery itself can guide your own ability to achieve this ideal state of mind.

Design, not chance, underlies both flow and focus. As I've pointed out, chance and the unconscious play prodigious roles in productive mental activity, but they make their best contributions when flowing freely with the least obstruction possible. It turns out—and this was the great discovery—that there actually is an overarching design in nature that creates most efficient movement of everything, from air to water to traffic to luggage to lightning to information to ideas, and yes, to attention.

Sometimes important ideas simply pop into a person's mind without any warning or preparation. This happens all the time in minor ways. We suddenly remember where we left our glasses or, out of nowhere, we are taken aback by an insight into a certain relationship we're in or an investment we're thinking of making. And sometimes, such spontaneous insights change our world. Although rare, the momentous *eureka!* moment does occur. Examples live in the mythology of our culture: Archimedes sitting in his bathtub, discovering displacement, or Newton sitting beneath the famous apple tree, discovering gravity. We don't know for sure if those two moments actually did happen, but they make for great stories.

However, I'm going to tell you about one *eureka!* moment that we know for sure did happen recently. We know about it because the man to whom it happened describes it in his 2012 book, *Design in Nature*.[8]

In September, 1995, Adrian Bejan, then a forty-seven-year-old professor of mechanical engineering at Duke University, traveled to Nancy, France, to give a lecture at a conference on thermodynamics, his field of specialization. Before he could give his lecture, something took place that we all dream of but rarely experience. It was something Bejan didn't plan or even intimate might occur, something that would change his life, and although it's too soon to tell, it was also something that quite possibly will change our understanding of the world.

At the preconference banquet, Ilya Prigogine, the Belgian Nobel laureate, gave a speech Bejan attended. During his talk, Prigogine made a statement that caught Bejan's attention. Indeed, it stopped him cold. If the apple ever did hit Newton's head, it hit with the same unique impact that Prigogine's remark hit Bejan.

Prigogine's remark was a commonplace statement, one that the entire scientific community agreed with at the time. He noted that while many treelike structures in nature—from lightning bolts, to the air ducts in lungs, to river deltas—resembled each other, they did so purely by chance, and for no reason other than chance. The fact that the structures resembled each other, Prigogine said, was mere coincidence. No unifying principle dictated either the abundance of such treelike designs through-out the world, or their congruity in vastly different contexts.

As Bejan put it, the moment Prigogine made that statement, "Some-thing clicked. The penny dropped. I knew that Prigogine, and everyone else, was wrong. In a flash I realized that the world was not formed by random accidents, chance, and fate but that behind the dizzying diver-sity is a seamless stream of predictable patterns."[9]

He then went on to write out, in longhand and on the spot, what he named the "constructal law": "For a finite-size flow system to persist in time (to live), its configuration must evolve in such a way that provides easier access to the currents that flow through it."[10] At first glance, at least to a nonengineer like me, this principle sounds unimportant and absurdly arcane, not remotely relevant to everyday life, and certainly not relevant to this book. But that first glance would be quite wrong.

Let me explain why. The constructal law is a law of physics that gov-erns all flow systems—which is to say any system, animate or inanimate, in which there is movement of any kind. The constructal law governs every system that we encounter, from traffic to sports to the makeup of organizations to birds in flight or fish in schools or, of course, the internet. Which is also to say that it governs not only all those systems, but also the system of neurons in the brain, and the flow of ideas those neurons carry.

In simple terms, the constructal law states that all flow systems—systems in which there is movement—evolve in such a way as to improve movement against resistance of any kind. Over time, the constructal law predicts that all systems must allow for ever-improving movement—water through the delta, air through the lungs, lightning from the cloud to the flagpole—or an idea from its inception to its expression.

If movement does not proceed more and more efficiently, movement will gradually cease. Perhaps that's one reason so many people stop thinking after they leave childhood. Their minds dam up everything, so that nothing moves forward and develops but, rather, recirculates. When movement ceases, so does life, which one might define as movement. No movement of any kind is death.

In Bejan's language of thermodynamics, death means that the system is at equilibrium with its surroundings. There is no movement in or out of it. This is thermodynamic death, but it might as well mean death, period. Life is movement or, to use Bejan's word, flow. A treelike structure is a marvelously effective design for allowing easy flow—of water, air, or electricity—from an area to a point or a point to an area. That's why nature seeks it and creates it.

Now, let's look at the brain. What, you might ask, is the design of the connecting junctures between neurons in the brain? The design of a tree, of course. As the long cell body (or trunk) of the nerve cell, or neuron, reaches its end, it splays out into dendrites (or branches), which receive incoming signals from adjacent neurons in the synapse. The very word, dendrite, is derived from the Greek word for tree.

I cite Bejan's moment of discovery to make two points. First, sometimes a great idea, like a great fish, will jerk on your line and all but pull you out of the boat. The great fisherman, like Bejan, is ready for it and so is able to reel it in, even when he least expects it to strike. Second, and far more important for us, Bejan's constructal law tells us that there is a pattern that will improve the flow of ideas. Even if we can't create it at will, just the fact that this pattern exists means we can take steps to increase its likelihood of taking shape.

We can take steps to increase the likelihood not only of great ideas finding our bait, but also of attention and thought flowing more efficiently through our conscious minds, even in the absence of a great idea.

In 1854, Louis Pasteur famously remarked in a lecture, *Dans les champs de l'observation le hasard ne favorise que les esprits préparés.*[11] Translation: "In the fields of observation, chance favors only the prepared mind." The question then becomes: How best to prepare your mind to allow for the most efficient flow of information and ideas?

The anatomy of your brain, made up of millions of dendrites all obeying the constructal law, does what it can. But you can help your brain by taking various steps of your own. There are specific, proven ways you can assist nature and anatomy in allowing for the most efficient flow of ideas. Rather than applying frantic effort in the acute moment, as if you are being reprimanded by a demonic fifth-grade teacher, you will achieve flexible focus by relying on planning, preparation, and technique. The most successful ways to sustain attention rely on habit and training, as is the case with just about anything else we want to master.

Much of what prevents us from mastering the magic of mental clarity is obstructed or diverted by the incessant input of ideas and information, and the kinds of self-sabotaging stories that we tell ourselves. Just as pollution has threatened real fishing, the pollution of our mental lives with excessive and sometimes toxic data, interruptions, memories, interpretations, and distractions threatens our ability to achieve flexible focus. To achieve that goal, we need to both limit the distractions and feed our minds and bodies with what they need. Just as a garden can't thrive without good soil, adequate sunlight, water, and constant weeding of the stuff that chokes out the vegetables and flowers, we can't achieve flexible focus if we don't do the fundamental work of caring for ourselves.

Before offering pointers on how to create the conditions that favor flexible focus and remove obstacles to movement of ideas and information through the mind, think to yourself, "What could I do to use the constructal law to help me focus more clearly and use my mind more fluently?" Or, put another way, since you know your situation better than anyone, ask yourself, "What are the obstacles to the free movement of information and ideas through my mind? And how can I remove those obstacles?"

For most people today, the obstacles could not be more obvious: ongoing distractions, nonstop interruptions, screen sucking, a multiplicity of opportunities and obligations, and a general overloading of mental circuits. Far from removing obstacles to the free flow of information and ideas through our minds, we often do the opposite. We clog up the channels. We create a mental traffic jam, precisely the opposite of what Bejan's constructal law would have us do.

However, it does not have to be that way. The jam can be cleared. Traffic can flow fast and free through the mind—if you make plans for it to do so.

the essential ingredients:
energy, emotion, engagement, structure, control

All the elements in the plan I've developed aim to remove obstacles so that, obeying the constructal law, the mind can connect unimpeded with its targets over extended periods of time. The basic plan provides for the most efficient, least obstructed flow of information and ideas in and out of the brain. The specifics I suggest from here on—from getting physical exercise, to creating the optimal emotional state, to reducing distractions, to finding and focusing in your "sweet spot"—all aim to improve movement and promote unimpeded flow.

So let's assume you have embarked on the psychological work of looking at your self-limiting patterns, possibly with the help of a trained professional, and that you are ready to detach yourself from the old stories and patterns that may have helped to protect you psychologically as a child, but now hold you back. Such work can take years, but it need not. If you stick with it, over time you will find that the old bad habits begin to loosen their hold. So let's assume you're ready to make some changes to help you achieve at your highest level.

In the next several chapters, I'll show you how you can train yourself in the practical habits that will lead you toward flexible focus. While the details that create flexible focus vary from person to person, some elements must appear in every plan, just as some ingredients are common to, say, all good red sauces. Many Italian cooks would say that tomatoes, in some form, olive oil, onions, garlic, and a choice of thyme, basil, or oregano are the five essential ingredients in a good red sauce. Some would add carrots, celery, and green peppers to the list, along with salt, pepper, and maybe sugar (not me!). But no cook would omit tomatoes, olive oil, and various seasonings.

It's the same with flexible focus. There are five essential elements in my basic recipe. I developed my recipe in the test kitchen of my own life and in my clinic with thousands of clients and patients over the past thirty-plus years. I savor the recipe because my moments of full attention, of flexible focus, are moments I enjoy even more than a fine wine or a sublime meal. In these moments, I make what amounts to mental music, and so do we all. If you think of consciousness as a violin, moments of flexible focus are when we play it the best. It is when the ideas and information are flowing against the least resistance.

The basic plan includes the following five key elements, which I described in the introduction. You will always need these five ingredients. You will add your own favorite flavorings to this basic set, but if any one of the five is missing, the plan will fail.

1. ENERGY. You should monitor your brain's energy supply at least as carefully as you monitor your car's supply of gas or your bank account's supply of money. You'll be surprised at how much more focused you can be every day if you follow the six basic practices of wise energy management, my so-called "sensational six" (sleep, nutrition, exercise, meditation, cognitive stimulation, and positive human contact), and how poorly focused you become when you neglect any of them.

2. EMOTION. Passion drives achievement. If you want to achieve flexible focus, you need to learn how to regulate your emotional

state. Emotion can be your greatest ally, but it can also hold you back more than your worst enemy. The secret is to work in an environment that is high on trust and low on fear, to work in a position that allows you to use your best talents, and to know your hot buttons and emotional foibles and learn to manage them well.

3. ENGAGEMENT. To perform at your best, you must get hooked or engaged. As Jim Loehr, one of the world's authorities on peak performance, points out, engagement, like a turbocharge, drives us to achieve at our best.[12] When you work in your sweet spot, the overlap of what you love to do and are really good at doing, and what advances the mission or what someone will pay you to do, you maximize your chances of getting hooked and fully engaged.

4. STRUCTURE. Structure, this simplest of words, has the most magnificent powers. It clears your way. It slashes through the underbrush. It allows you to focus rather than constantly being led off track. Structure refers to the world you create for yourself, the work world you build. It also refers to what you do, rather than what you let be done to you. Flexible focus depends upon structure, and structure depends upon planning and taking back the control you may have unwittingly given away.

5. CONTROL. The entire five-step plan depends upon your exercising what control you have, rather than allowing modern life to control you. People have varying levels of control, depending on their situations, but most people today have *far* more control than they use.

In the chapters that follow, I will outline various elements of the plan in more detail. As you learn to work with yourself rather than against yourself, to work with your grain rather than against it, to create strategies that facilitate focus and peak performance, to learn remedies beyond the old standby of simply working harder, you will indeed find that the seemingly magical process yields to rational planning and produces extraordinary results.

harnessing the power of the body

How many times have you found yourself sitting in a meeting, yawning, pinching yourself, grinding your teeth, or chewing your tongue in a painful effort to stay awake? (Note: your tongue doesn't love this.) How many days have you gone to the coffee machine multiple times, begging the caffeine to create some extra energy? (Note: don't rely on caffeine. It can help, but it can't do the whole job.)

Most people wake up, maybe grab some breakfast or at least a shot of caffeine, go to work, and assume they can stay consistently focused without doing any special preparation or taking any steps specifically designed to replenish and maintain their energy throughout the day. Such people are exhibit A in poor mental-energy management. If you are such a person, don't feel bad; after all, few people, and certainly few managers, teach anyone how to regulate mental energy. Starbucks, Dunkin' Donuts, Red Bull, Mountain Dew, Jolt, and the local drug dealer all love your ignorance, but your brain and the rest of your body don't. And when your brain is in a bad way, you perform poorly.

Rule number one is this: never take energy for granted. You can't be alert if your energy is low, and you can't pay a nickel's worth of attention if you aren't alert. Low energy means low focus. High energy is a necessary, albeit insufficient, condition for high focus. You can get through the day, as most people do, without taking special care of your energy supply, but if you want to do better than just get through, then follow the simple steps I lay out in this and the chapters that follow. Over time, they will ensure optimal maintenance of energy for your brain.

Every day in the newspaper, on the internet, or in the thousands of books about the brain now in print, you can read about ways to overhaul yourself by overhauling your brain. Some of these plans are sound, while others aim only to sell you a line of products. I've tested many of the products on myself, and if nothing else, they've given me the most expensive urine in the Boston area. You truly do not need most of what's for sale. Brain boosters have become the nutritional equivalent of cosmetics: people pay tons of money for the products, not because they are actually getting something of value, but because they want to believe they are.

It's amazing how many of us disregard something as important and simple as personal energy management until we are practically somnolent, on the brink of conking out, or making serious, serial mistakes. But here is a simple, important fact: your body knows things that your brain doesn't. Your body knows your energy state before your brain does; it's as if your body has a brain, too. You can't be on top of your game, produce what you need to produce, focus, and learn if your body—of which your brain is obviously a part—isn't primed to do it.

Over a century ago, William James posited that the mind follows the body's commands, not the other way around. More recently, social psychologist James Laird ran an experiment in which he attached electrodes to people's faces and directed some to smile, others to frown. Then he asked the people how they felt. The smilers felt happier, and the frowners felt angrier.[1] In other words, what's going on biologically—in your body—goes a long way in determining how and what you feel and think.

For something this important, managing your physical and mental energy is pretty simple, though doing so may require some changes of habit. There are two components of effective energy management. First, and by far most important, is preparation, or what I call prep work—making your entire self able to support you as you go about your day. Second is maintenance throughout the day, or what I call field work. Most people pay far more attention to field work—intervening in the moment of crisis or fatigue—than prep work, which would prevent the crisis and fatigue from occurring in the first place.

the sensational six

Prep work relies on "the sensational six." Do the things I recommend in this and succeeding chapters, and your body and brain will love you. Your brain will give you much more time in flexible focus if you prepare it every day by following each of these practices.

As you read through the next two chapters, you might be tempted to say, "Yes, yes, I know all that already." And you may. But do you use what you know? The key now is for you to start practicing the sensational six in your daily life so that your body and brain can support you as you work and play. As I mentioned before, these are the practices:

- Sleep

- Nutrition

- Exercise

- Meditation

- Stimulation

- Connection (positive human contact)

We all need to follow the first three practices (sleep, nutrition, and exercise) in order to function and stay healthy. The second two (meditation, stimulation) boost psychological health as well as physical. We often overlook or avoid the last one, connection. It is my proprietary element, the one that I champion above all others, while most other experts ignore it or fail to recognize its extraordinary power.

These six practices interweave and support each other. The greatest power lies in following all six.

sleep

Remember Jean, who illustrated the problem of multitasking? One reason her focus was chronically splintered had to do with her inability to get enough sleep. Try as she might, she never was able to create a schedule that allowed her to get the sleep her brain and body needed to function optimally. And remember Jack, who illustrated the problem of excessive worry? He dismissed sleep by saying, "I can sleep when I'm dead." He paid a far greater price than he realized for his cavalier attitude.

Like Jean and Jack, millions of people operate on too little sleep, and they hurt themselves in big and small ways as a result. If you regularly get less than whatever your body needs, the levels of the appetite-increasing hormone, ghrelin, rise, while the levels of the appetite-suppressing hormone, leptin, decline. That's why lack of sleep can make you fat. Sleeplessness also contributes to high blood pressure, depressed immune function, and an increased risk of cancer and of catching colds and flu. It is also well known that lack of sleep leads to irritability, trouble concentrating, and lapses in memory. Lack of sleep turns highways into danger zones. Roughly 60 percent of adult drivers report having driven a vehicle while feeling drowsy in the space of a year, and more than a third say they have actually fallen asleep at the wheel—putting themselves, their passengers, and other drivers in serious jeopardy.[2] As if that weren't enough, lack of sleep makes your face puffy and unattractive.

Moreover, it's practically impossible to get into a state of flexible focus if you are sleep deprived. In fact, in a sleep-deprived state, you're likely to develop ADHD-like symptoms. In an April 2013 *New York Times* article, Dr. Vatsal Thakkar described a patient who "had all the classic symptoms of ADHD: procrastination, forgetfulness, a propensity to lose things, and, of course, the inability to pay attention consistently." Weirdly, the patient was thirty-one and had never had these symptoms before, something that went completely against the diagnostic criteria for ADHD. As it turned out, the patient had a chronic sleep deficit, not ADHD. After the doctor prescribed some techniques for getting to sleep at night, the patient's symptoms disappeared.[3]

One of the greatest favors you can do your brain and your entire body is to get enough sleep. Sleep is tonic. As Shakespeare observed, sleep "knits up the raveled sleeve of care, the death of each day's life, sore labor's bath, balm of hurt minds, great nature's second course, chief nourisher in life's feast." Shakespeare knew that sleep is really good for you. "I don't disagree," you may respond, "but I just don't have time to get the sleep I should get. I have too much work to do and, if I'm going to see my family at all, the hours I'd otherwise spend sleeping are the only place where I can steal time for the work I have to get done."

Reset your priorities to make time for sleep. Science has proven it's worth it. Sleep research has been booming of late, which, in a recent book, journalist David K. Randall engagingly summarizes:

> Today's researchers believe that they are in the golden age of their field. Sleep is now understood as a complex process that affects everything from the legal system to how babies are raised to how a soldier returning from war recovers from trauma. And it

is also seen as a vital part of happiness. Whether you realize it or not, how you slept last night probably has a bigger impact on your life than what you decide to eat, how much money you make, or where you live. All of those things that add up to what you consider you—your creativity, emotions, health, and ability to quickly learn a new skill or devise a solution to a problem—can be seen as little more than by-products of what happens inside your brain while your head is on a pillow each night. It is part of a world that all of us enter and yet barely understand . . . Sleep isn't a break from our lives. It's the missing third of the puzzle of what it means to be living.[4]

The amount of sleep you need varies from person to person. One way to tell how much you need is to notice how long you sleep without being awakened by an alarm clock or some other external means of waking you up. Assuming you don't drink alcohol before you go to bed (alcohol is a sleep disrupter), and you aren't overtired so that you are in catch-up mode, your body will tell you how much sleep you physiologically need by waking you up when you've reached that number of hours. Most adults need between seven and eight hours of sleep a night. A few of us need less, and some of us more.

Whatever you do, please don't think of sleep as wasted time, an indulgence, or a generous reservoir from which you can steal time for work. Do what your brain and body beg you to do: get enough sleep. To do this, you will need to develop new habits if you don't get enough sleep now. In the short run, you will need discipline, but you will reap rewards quickly, which will solidify your motivation. As an immediate payoff, you will wake up refreshed and sharp, rather than needing to push the snooze button. You will feel what I call a "morning burst," a surge of energy that can power some of your best work right at the start of the day.

You can make the process easier by practicing what's called good sleep hygiene. Here are a few do's and don'ts:

- Do set a regular bedtime and get-up time. Your brain gets used to this.

- Do make sure you have comfortable bedding.

- Do reserve your bed for sleep and sex, not for work.

- Do turn off the TV and take a warm bath or read a bit before sleep.

- Don't drink alcohol for four hours before sleep. Alcohol induces sleep at first, but then as levels decline, it wakes you up during the night and interferes with valuable REM sleep.

- Don't eat heavy foods for four hours before sleep.

- Don't engage in heavy exercise before sleep.

- Don't toss and turn if you can't sleep. Instead, get up and go into another room and read for a little while.

Most people sleep better if they don't share a bed. If you sleep poorly, you might consider sleeping alone or getting a king-size bed. If your partner snores, wakes up during the night, or tosses and turns, you won't get the sleep you need. A January 1991 study published in the *Journal of Marital & Family Therapy* found that spouses that had opposite sleep-wake patterns reported more difficulties in their relationship, including less frequent sex, less time talking, and more conflict overall.[5]

A nap in mid-afternoon, the typical time people feel sleepy, can provide a quick pick-me-up. Some enlightened companies actually set aside "nap rooms" that people can sign up for. If napping is not for you, consider meditation, which can be just as helpful as a nap.[6]

If sleep continues to be a problem, you might consider playing soothing music as you fall asleep. There is a free app called Dreampad that can download to your smartphone. I use it myself; it always puts my wife and me to sleep! And there are various natural sleep remedies, like valerian root and melatonin, as well as over-the-counter sleep aids such as Benadryl or Tylenol PM. Finally, there are prescription sleep remedies like Ambien, Lunesta, and Trazodone. I strongly advise using the prescription aids only as a last resort. People reach for them too quickly and become dependent on them rather than practicing proper sleep hygiene and using natural aids.

Consult with your doctor regarding ongoing sleep problems, as there are various medical and psychiatric problems that can interfere with sleep, including sleep apnea, depression, anxiety disorders, arthritis, cancer, heart failure, lung disease, gastroesophageal reflux disease (GERD), over-active thyroid, stroke, Parkinson's disease, and Alzheimer's disease, as well as medications or medical conditions that wake you up to urinate. Don't diagnose yourself. When you see your doctor, try to come away with better solutions than medication alone. Remember Mary, whose doctor gave her Prozac, saying simply, "At least it's something," when she needed much more help than just that. You should always have a multimodal approach to problems related not just to sleep, but to the mind-brain in general.

nutrition

As the people I profiled in part I began to sink into trouble, most of them encountered problems with nutrition. Some people self-medicate with food, as Jean did, when they are stressed or anxious. Some people go in the other direction and starve themselves. Les substituted life in front of a screen for a healthy diet, and it cost him.

Nutrition is a hot topic these days, and justifiably so. Last time I checked, there were 229,384 books related to food on Amazon.com. Diet books abound. The subject of nutrition has moved from a topic of marginal interest a few decades ago to the mainstream today. At your average social gathering, you will usually hear at least a few people talking about the "cleansing regimen" they just went on, or the supplement they're taking and swear by, or the surprisingly tasty vegan selections at the spa they just returned from.

To avoid wasting money (at best) and putting one's life in danger (at worst), it's critical that the buyer be informed. No longer a minor fad, nutrition is a science whose time has come, and we need to take this science seriously. At one time, we didn't need to monitor so carefully what we ate, as well as what we breathed in, what we drank, what came into contact with our skin, and what hit us through invisible currents of radiation or other forms of energy from the sun, power lines, television screens, cellphones, and who knows what else. But that time is past.

To achieve health today, we must monitor what gets into us, by whatever route. It's said we are what we eat. Also include in that what we breathe, touch, absorb, or in any other way take in. While we can't control all the routes of access into ourselves, we can regulate what we eat and drink, as long as we take care to do so.

When you don't eat right, your brain can't function well. Many people wake up in the morning, drink a cup or two of coffee and eat a bagel or muffin, and call that breakfast, or eat nothing at all. Then they eat a big sandwich and a bag of Doritos for lunch, down it with a sugar-packed soda, and wonder why they feel sleepy in the afternoon (this is about eating high-glycemic food, to which I'll turn in a moment). Later, they go home and eat a hamburger, have a beer or three, and relax in front of the television. Note the lack of fruits and vegetables. While the pounds pile on, the brain, depleted of the real nutrition it needs to function well, is starving.

You simply can't focus when you're in a starch-and-sugar induced haze. You have to eat, so why not eat as healthfully as you can so you can do your best work? It is beyond the scope of this book to give detailed advice on what makes for the healthiest diet. However, I would like to stress a few basic points.

Like getting enough sleep, eating the right food is not difficult to do, unless you live in poverty. If you are reading this book, you can probably afford to eat right. Like sleeping right, it is mostly a matter of learning what's best, then committing to doing it.

Before focusing in on nutrition and the brain, let me first emphasize a few principles of sound nutrition in general and offer a few specific suggestions as well:

- EAT WHOLE FOODS. Avoid packaged, processed, or preserved foods. With some exceptions, like canned tomatoes, the food that is best for you is fresh from the ground, the farm, or the sea. The China Study, one of the most rigorous studies ever conducted on what makes for the healthiest diet, concluded that vegan was best. The scientists who conducted the study examined the eating habits in over 100 villages across China. While vegan was best, it was also clear that eating plenty of vegetables and whole foods in general correlated with good health.[7] If you can't or don't want to do vegan (I can't and, on most days, don't want to), then come as close as you can.

- ABSORB THE NUTRIENTS YOU INGEST. Many people begin the day with a cup of warm water and a squeeze of lemon to help their bodies digest food better. A middle-aged friend of mine also noticed a big difference when she began making her own fresh, blended juice. She bought a powerful juicer into which she tosses whole fruits (blueberries, apples, half a banana, half a lemon), vegetables (carrots, cucumber, spinach, ginger). She adds a tablespoon of Spirulina, a tablespoon of protein powder, a packet of the natural sweetener stevia, water, and presses the whoosh button. "I drink it in the morning and snack on it through the day," she says. "I eat a healthy salad for lunch and a small dinner. The week I began doing this, I noticed a gigantic jump in my energy, focus, and productivity. And I've lost weight, too!"

- KEEP RED MEAT TO A MINIMUM. If you must eat red meat, consider buying organic and grass-fed beef, buffalo, or venison. Use fish, pork, chicken, beans, and other nutrient-rich vegetables as a source of nourishment instead. Don't scarf down a whole steak; instead, broil one, cut off a quarter, and use it as a salad topping. Many would advise omitting not only beef, but pork, chicken, and even fish (I eat them, but it's your call).

- CONSIDER GOING GLUTEN-FREE. I went gluten-free myself and lost twenty pounds I needed to lose in six weeks, pounds that have stayed off. I feel more mentally alert than before as well. It may seem like a major change, but I found it not all that hard to go gluten-free. You just give up anything that contains wheat, malt, rye, and bulgur, which means you give up most bread, cake, cookies, crackers, pasta, beer, soy sauce, and various other foods.[8]

- CONSIDER ELIMINATING DAIRY. Some experts urge removing all dairy from milk to cheese to ice cream from your diet. (A nutritionist I know and respect has been trying to persuade me to eliminate dairy, but as yet, I haven't. You can be your own laboratory; try it and see how you feel.)

- EAT LOCALLY. Try to eat locally raised food free of hormones, antibiotics, pesticides, and other chemicals. If you have read the eye-opening book *Fast Food Nation* or have seen the chilling, award-winning documentary *Food, Inc.*, you already know that you should avoid all food produced by mass marketers, all the well-known brands, and stick with sources of food you know well enough to trust. The hormones, preservatives, and other chemicals that what I call "Big Farma" (the agricultural version of Big Pharma) put into food can slowly poison us, and they can block the body's ability to absorb nutrients. It makes sense to eat only those foods you know do not contain harmful chemicals, additives, or contaminants. Research your food, where it comes from and what goes into it, wherever you shop. If you can, put in a few raised beds in your backyard and grow your own fresh veggies and fruits. If you can't, just buy food you know is good.

- TAKE THE RIGHT SUPPLEMENTS. According to the April 2012 issue of the *Harvard Men's Health Watch*, half the adult population takes at least one dietary supplement.[9] Because supplements are not regulated by the FDA, they are far easier to market than medications. Often cheap to produce, they turn huge profits. In 2010, Americans spent $28 billion on supplements. Most of these purchases were rooted more in blind hope and persuasive, deceptive advertising than in scientific evidence. According to the same Harvard report, even multivitamins are not worth the money we spend on them. For adults, the Harvard report advises a daily supplement of vitamin D3, 1,000 international units, or IU; along with a daily supplement of calcium carbonate or calcium citrate, 1,000 milligrams for men, higher levels for women; as well as a daily supplement of 1,000 milligrams of omega-3 fatty acids, DHA, and EPA. You should consult with your doctor before committing to any of these, but in most instances, your doctor will approve. If you carefully follow each of my suggestions for good nutrition, your body will be better able to absorb the nutrients it needs anyway, so you won't need supplements.

Taking these steps is no longer just for tree huggers and fanatics. All of us ought to do it for our health in general and our mental acuity in particular.

There is one other critical food you should monitor throughout the day to help your brain stay focused and alert—glucose. Glucose is the brain's chief source of energy. If glucose levels remain steady throughout the day, you stand the best chance of maintaining constant focus.

Unfortunately, many people eat in such a way that their glucose levels yo-yo up and down. When you start your day with coffee and a muffin or a bagel, your pancreas secretes a bolus of insulin to handle the sugar (glucose) load. Your blood glucose level spikes, then plummets when the insulin hits its targets. As glucose levels plummet, you head to the coffee station for more caffeine and carbohydrates to get more energy, which induces the cycle to repeat over and over throughout the day.

Ever wonder why there's a Starbucks or Dunkin' Donuts on every block? And why they sell the combination of caffeine and foods packed with sugar? Because they are cashing in on this cycle. The caffeine-and-carbs dealers are the most dangerous purveyors of legal drugs on the planet, mostly because so few people are aware of the dangers.

After lunch, especially a lunch high in starchy carbohydrates and low in protein, the same spike and trough in glucose ensues, leading to the well-known 3 p.m. blahs. You might think that you are just not an afternoon person or you might wish you could live in a country where an afternoon siesta is the norm. Instead, you can avoid the mid-afternoon blahs simply by eating a lunch that has enough protein to help stabilize your glucose level. If you do feel some blahs, simply do a brief burst of exercise, followed by eating an apple or a banana—or some of that left-over homemade juice—or take a quick nap.

The general rule in connecting nutrition to brain function throughout the day is: do all you can to keep your glucose level from yo-yoing. Eat a breakfast with protein. Eat a balanced lunch. Use a fruit snack and a burst of exercise to combat the blahs. Eat more fresh fruits and veg-etables to feed your brain the micronutrients it needs.

Also, watch the amount of coffee you drink. Like Jack, who was a caffeine addict, billions of people around the world use caffeine every day. By any sensible reckoning, caffeine is a performance-enhancing drug. (One study showed that women who drank four cups of coffee per day had a significantly lower risk of depression than those who did not.)[10] Used wisely, caffeine is an ally. A cup of coffee increases your ability to focus and think quickly. Just don't drink too much of it or rely on caffeine, rather than the other steps in the sensational six to maintain your mental energy.

How much is too much? If you have undesirable side effects like elevated blood pressure, elevated heart rate, agitation and anxiety, upset stomach, headache, dizziness, or insomnia, that's too much. Caffeine is a diuretic, which means it will make you urinate more than usual, but that is an acceptable side effect within reasonable limits. It can also act as a laxative, which, again, is acceptable within limits. Be careful of abruptly discontinuing the use of caffeine. If you don't gradually taper it, you will get a severe headache.

The takeaway on caffeine: some is good, too much is bad. I drink two or three cups of coffee a day. It is my favorite medication to help me focus. I rarely leave home without it.

exercise

The people profiled in part I encountered their periods of greatest success when they were physically active. Think of Jack and how happy—and successful—he was in college when he was playing Division I hockey. Or think what a godsend the world of sport was for Sharon as she was growing up.

That physical exercise enhances brain function is now well documented. For example, in 2011, a team of researchers at the University of Illinois conducted an experiment with four groups of mice. One group lived like little princelings: they got to eat nuts, fruits, and cheese, and lived in cages filled with colorful toys. Another group got the same treatment, but also had small running wheels in the cages. In the third group's cage, the poor mice got nothing but boring kibble and water and some bedding. The fourth group's cage was as sparse as the third's, but it included a running wheel. The researchers then put the mice through some cognitive tests and studied their brain tissues. It turned out that the toys and fancy food did not improve the mice's brainpower. The only variable that made a significant difference was the running wheel. The mice that ran on the wheel had healthier brains and did better on cognitive tests than the mice that did not have access to the running wheel.[11]

If you need further convincing on the extraordinary power of exercise to revitalize your life, replenish your brain, and restore your zest, read the book, *Spark: The Revolutionary New Science of Exercise and the Brain*, by my close friend and colleague, John Ratey, MD. In the book, Ratey explains how exercise is truly the best defense against everything from mood disorders to ADHD, addiction, menopause, and Alzheimer's disease. He demonstrates how the brain works exactly like the body's muscles do; they grow stronger with use and atrophy with inactivity. The data underlying his research is conclusive.[12] Exercise is beyond doubt one of the best tonics available for your brain. If we all got enough exercise, we could quickly and drastically reduce our use of medications not only in psychiatry but in medicine in general.

I can hear you thinking, "I get it. I should get on the treadmill." But that idea bores you to death. Mice actually like running wheels, but for most humans, including myself, even the thought of such exercise is an instant turnoff. It's no fun. It's time consuming. You sweat, and you stink, and even when you do it, you have little to show for it, compared to all those fabulously fit runners and lifters. You've finally given up on ever becoming one of them, one of those supreme achievers who has a perfect body and is training for the Iron Man Triathlon in Hawaii. What to do?

The secret is: *make it fun*. Start by walking every day with a friend. Find someone else who wants to make exercise a regular part of his or her life, and schedule a morning walk or an evening stroll. If one of you has a dog, all the better. If it's winter, just dress warmly. Another way to incorporate exercise into your life is by reserving time for a game of some sort. I've been playing squash on Tuesday afternoons with my best friend for thirty-two years. It's a great way to both get exercise, and also keep up with a friend (which is really good for your brain, too).

A third way, which is more expensive than the previous two (both of which are free), is to work with a trainer. The great thing about a trainer is that, since you are paying him or her, you tend to show up, while the trainer sees to it that you don't slack off.

In 2003, I had a total hip replacement (all those years of playing squash caught up with me). After I went through the weeks of rehab, I started working out with a Russian trainer named Simon Zaltsman, who has changed my life. Zaltsman is in his sixties and built like the proverbial brick outhouse. He is both a world-class mathematician and a world-class athlete. Ever since he came to the United States, he's worked as a trainer.

What is so special about Zaltsman is that he is smart and has such a wry, low-key sense of humor, that, as tired as I get during the workouts, I am never bored. For example, in our very first workout, he had me do some weight lifting. At one point, I groaned in protest, "Oh, God!" In his rich Russian accent, Zaltsman mordantly replied, "Gud cannot halp you now."

Even though I am lazy and hate exercise for the sake of exercise, I look forward to going to my sessions with Zaltsman. I know he will keep me amused even as I endure what he likes to call "good torture." And the sessions have stood me in good stead, for in 2013, I had my other hip replaced. I rebounded much faster from the operation in 2013 than the one in 2003, thanks to my work with Zaltsman.

One last point. Remember, sex counts as exercise. Sex raises your heartbeat and metabolism; it floods your brain with oxygen and your body with all kinds of beneficial hormones. Orgasms are good for you. Best of all, sex is fun. So enjoy as much sex as you can (with a consenting partner, of course). Sex is one of the few things in life that is good for you, you're born with the ability to do, is free, and is fun.

harnessing the power of the mind

Allow me to tell you a story about how I finally overcame my addiction to tobacco. In 1990, I decided that I could wait no longer; I simply *had* to quit smoking. I'd smoked since high school and had wanted to quit for years, but when my daughter Lucy came into my life, quitting smoking became imperative.

I tried going cold turkey several times, and each time I relapsed. Then I went to a guru people in Boston called "the mad Russian." He hypnotized large audiences to help them quit smoking and had great results. While he had a stellar reputation and his hypnotic suggestions worked wonders for many people, the mad Russian's efforts did nothing for me except lighten my wallet.

Next, I went to see a behaviorist who *guaranteed* that I would quit as long as I followed his instructions to the letter. (I am a sucker for guarantees.) He instructed me as follows: "You may smoke as much as you want to. However, for your next cigarette, you must put one cent into a special account to be donated to your favorite charity. For the next cigarette, two cents, and for the third, you pay four cents. The price doubles for each successive cigarette. Smoke as many as you like, just double the price each time you light up a new one." If you do the arithmetic, you'll see that for my mere thirtieth cigarette, I'd be giving my charity $5,368,709.12. For obvious reasons, I was not able to follow the behaviorist's instructions. I felt ashamed. I felt like a bad person, an addict, a weak man, a lousy husband, and a lousy dad.

Then I went to see an acupuncturist. I feared the needles, but I was willing to suffer whatever pain it took to quit. To my absolute astonishment, I loved the experience of getting stuck. The insertion of the filament-sized needles released an endorphin high. I would lie on the doctor's table and drift to sweet places, listening to soft music. I looked forward to my appointments and went religiously twice a week for twelve weeks. I loved acupuncture! But I didn't quit smoking.

However, acupuncture whetted my appetite for getting that wonderful feeling the needles induced. I'd heard that both long-distance running and meditation could produce similar effects. Since I'm lazy, I was about as likely to learn Mandarin as take up long-distance running, so I thought I'd give meditation a try.

Meditation worked. I quit smoking. I have not had a cigarette in over twenty years.

meditation

You've heard about the myriad benefits of meditation—that it can lower stress levels and blood pressure, increase energy and cognitive function, and make you calmer and happier. But meditation does much more than that. Aside from helping me give up my addiction to nicotine, meditation has helped people in other wondrous ways. Recent research has shown that it helps a person function better psychologically. People who struggle with anxiety, addiction, depression, and eating disorders have benefited from it. It can even enhance leadership skills. In a wonderful book called *The Mindful Leader*, Michael Carroll lays out a program to help executives develop their management skills through meditation.[1]

My hope here is not to repeat what is already well known, but to convince you to incorporate some meditative practices into your daily life, if you have not already done so, and then to offer resources where you can learn all you need to get started. When I suggest that someone try meditating, I usually hear objections like the following: "Right," the person will say, with a roll of the eyeballs. "I know about meditation. I know it's an ancient practice. I know that smart people pay lots of money to go on 'retreats' where they sit on cushions for days, even weeks, eating only water and grains. I know it would be good for me to do that, too, just as a daily dose of wheat grass juice would be good for me along with a two-week cleanse. Sorry, but I'm just not up for it. I like hot dogs with mustard and I like nachos with oozy yellow cheese, and I'd rather relax by watching TV than by meditating. Honestly, hell will freeze over before I take up meditation."

I used to feel that way about flossing, and now I floss every day. I started flossing every day when I asked my dentist if I really did need to floss. He replied, "You only need to floss the teeth you want to keep." So I started flossing for real. I should do it twice a day, but I only do it once. On the other hand, I now meditate one or two times a day, not because I should, but *because it feels so good*. As an added benefit, I know it's really good for me. To my surprise, I like it so much that I've learned several different practices.

The core of most meditative practices couldn't be simpler. You sit in a comfortable chair in a room free from distraction. You put both feet on the floor and both hands on the arms of the chair or place them comfortably on your lap. You then close your eyes and focus on your breathing. In, out. In, out. You watch your thoughts float by like leaves on a river. You try not to evaluate your thoughts, but rather let them pass by indifferently, without a comment or a care. You detach as much as you can from conscious engagement with anything other than your focus on your breathing and the disinterested watching of whatever passes through your mind.

That's meditation. Most serious practitioners of meditation do it for stretches of twenty minutes or more, but if you just do it two or three times a day for as little as three to five minutes each time, you will feel better than you felt before, you will focus better, and your vital signs (blood pressure, heart rate, respiratory rate, and body temperature) will be lower.

There are thousands of good books from which you can learn how to meditate. In addition to the one I already mentioned, which is aimed at managers, two others I recommend are *Get Some Headspace: How Mindfulness Can Change Your Life in Ten Minutes a Day*, by Andy Puddicombe, and *The Mindfulness Prescription for Adult ADHD*, by Lidia Zylowska, MD. (You do not need to have ADHD to gain great benefit from this book.) Not only are the methods recommended in both easy to implement, both programs have been carefully researched and proven to work to enhance the focus of anyone who uses them, as well as provide the many other health benefits of meditation.

stimulation

Just as meditating is good for both your body and your brain, mental stimulation confers various benefits as well. When you stretch your brain by trying new tasks or doing everyday tasks in ways you've never done them before, you are doing something that will not only enhance your ability to maintain focus, but also help stave off the ravages of aging, including dementia.

One of the most obvious ways to stretch your brain is to take lessons in something that you've never done before. A friend of mine in her fifties who knew very little about music decided to take up piano. She told me that, in learning to read music, she felt as if her brain was "on fire" from the stimulation. Another friend who has mastered several foreign languages talks about the same feeling every time she learns a new one.

You can also take courses for free on "massive open online courses" (MOOCs) taught by famous professors and offered through elite universities like Harvard, MIT, Johns Hopkins, and UC Berkeley. (For a directory, go to www.MOOCs.com.) Alternatively, you can go online and listen to an illuminating TED talk. You can also go to one of the many online sites that serve as "brain gyms," like Lumosity or NeuroNation, where you can give your brain a workout.

You can also play various computer games to enhance various cognitive functions. For example, Cogmed, which has a solid base of research, improves active working memory, the amount of data you can hold in your mind at one time and work with. If you play (it's actually hard work!) Cogmed for a half hour or so, five days a week for five weeks, you are all but guaranteed to see a spike in active working memory. Or you can try the emWave from HeartMath. Another product backed by research, the emWave reduces anxiety and promotes superior performance.

In a recent *New Yorker* article, Patricia Marx wrote a highly informative and amusing review of these and similar products, while also reporting on her own experience using one of them, BrainHQ. While, as she put it, she didn't emerge "smart enough to date Harold Bloom," she did both enjoy much of the experience and also derive significant benefits, which the founder of BrainHQ, Michael Merzenich, told her "should last several years," after which she could slip back, or sign up for another training.[2]

Of course, there are plenty of other ways to stretch your brain. If you've only driven cars with automatic shifts, try learning to drive a car with a manual transmission. If you're right-handed, try writing (or mousing)

TABLE 9-1

Mental stimulation game board

17	4	5	12	22
8	1	11	16	3
2	20	14	19	7
18	24	9	10	13
21	6	15	25	23

with your left hand. Or try drawing a circle with one hand, a square with the other hand, and triangles with both feet. (This is not easy!)

Make a habit of challenging your brain and training your attentional systems. Here's one brain booster you can produce with the aid of your word processing program. Draw a grid with twenty-five boxes. Print it out, then put in the numbers one through twenty-five randomly, one in each box (see table 9-1).

Then take a pen or pencil and, starting with one, tap each number in sequence, one through twenty-five, as fast as you can. Time yourself and then do it again, this time in reverse order, twenty-five down to one. You can print out ten such grids and fill numbers into a blank grid as soon as you've done the previous one enough times that you know where the numbers are. It's an excellent exercise for training attention and flexing your brain.

Here's another exercise. Look at your desk, then look away. On a blank piece of paper, draw a replica of your desk that includes everything on it. You can make it more challenging by looking at a colleague's desk, then doing the same thing. Or at home, you can open a cupboard, stare inside for a minute, then close it and write down as many items as you can remember.

John F. Kennedy used to play a game when he was waiting for a play to start or a plane to take off. Write down seven random letters in a vertical column. Then across from each write down seven more random letters. For example one such grid could look like this:

F. N.

B. P.

N. L.

E. C.

M. M.

R. W.

T. A.

Look at each pair of letters as a famous person's initials and fill in as many as you can. For example, F. N. might be Florence Nightingale. E. C. might be E. E. Cummings. And M. M. might be Marilyn Monroe. I filled those in because I could think of them right away. See if you can do the rest. (I put one set of possible answers in an endnote.)[3] You can make this game tougher by trying to come up with a second name for each set of initials. Or, you can make it really tough by adding a third column and come up with a first, middle, and last name.

Of course, there are crossword puzzles and the loathsome Sudoku (I say loathsome because I am so bad at those). There are a plethora of websites devoted to cognitive stimulation and brain training. How much is a plethora? A Google search for "online cognitive stimulation sites" yielded 6.4 million entries. On Amazon, "brain games" brought 8,038 titles, while "cognitive stimulation" brought up 2,267. Once you get the basic idea, though, it's fun to make up your own games. That in itself becomes a form of cognitive stimulation.

Another powerful tool I use when I write is music. For years, I've listened to classical music while writing. My theory is that the music engages the part of my brain that would otherwise be distracting me. A British rock musician turned scientist of sound has taken that theory to a scientifically validated level. He has created music engineered *not* to engage the listener. Amazingly, if you listen to this music while, say, writing, your focus improves significantly. I now swear by it. I am listening to his music as I write these lines. If you want to try it, go to the website focusatwill.com. I predict you will be as impressed by it as I am.

harnessing the power of the human connection

The human connection is the most powerful force in the world for growth, health, fulfillment, and joy. At its most distilled, we call it love. As it spreads out, I call it *connection*, a feeling of being a part of something beneficent that is larger than oneself.

As powerful as connection is, it is typically relegated to some sentimental bin, trivialized, and dismissed as puny when compared to the supposedly more muscular drivers of excellence like rigor, discipline, sacrifice, and, of course, hard work. While those always matter, they lose much of their power unless used in a context of connection.

To cite Matthew Lieberman again: "People often talk as if their company, job, or workplace is solely about getting a paycheck and helping the company increase profits. This conversation is predicated on the norm of self-interest—the belief that self-interest is the only thing that motivates people . . . We have been bombarded with this idea for so long that it's the only conversation we know how to have about the workplace. But it is the wrong conversation to be having because it misses so much of what actually makes us us."[1] The conversation we ought to be having, that we are wired to be having, as Lieberman's research proves, is the conversation about connection.

the forgotten key

Developing connections of various kinds, not only human but inanimate as well (e.g., connection to a poem, to a favorite chair, to a meadow or a lake, to an idea or a creed, to a goal, to a tradition) is the cheapest, most effective step a person can take not only toward promoting mental clarity and focus, but toward promoting health, happiness, and productivity. It's that simple. *Nothing in life produces more that is good than the force of connection.* And nothing produces more misery than the force of disconnection.

I call connection "the other vitamin C," or "vitamin connect." It is as essential for life as the first vitamin C, ascorbic acid. Without that vitamin C, people die of a disease called scurvy. Without vitamin connect, people suffer, and not just emotionally, but physically as well.

Consider the case of the children who lived in orphanages during the reign of Romanian dictator Nicolae Ceaușescu, who was ousted from power in 1989. Because birth control was outlawed, many parents gave up their unwanted children to horrible institutions where the children weren't coddled or cuddled; there weren't enough caretakers. All the children were forced to eat, bathe, and go to the toilet at the same time. Babies were left in wet diapers and developed terrible rashes. Kids who acted out were tied to their cribs, dozens to a room. Researchers later found that the brains of these children had less white matter, or the important fat-covered tracts between brain cell bodies, than those who went into foster care.[2]

Then think of what happens to prisoners, the elderly, the mentally ill, and others who suffer from a lack of vitamin connect. People lacking connection descend a slow slope into the process of dying, and they die a death that rarely is named for what it is. The cause of death listed on the death certificate is usually cancer, stroke, heart attack, infection, or some other proximate cause. But those diseases represent the final common pathway of a much longer, insidious process initiated by loneliness, depression, lethargy, and lassitude, all brought on by a feeling of disconnection.

Lest you doubt that a lack of vitamin connect is fatal, consider the research of Lisa Berkman, a professor at the Harvard School of Public Health. Berkman led studies that rocked the world of academic medicine. First published in the 1970s, her research proved that social isolation poses as dangerous a risk factor for early death as cigarette smoking, obesity, or high blood pressure. At first, experts doubted the studies, but now her findings have been replicated around the world and can be considered fact. The first social scientist to prove the link between isolation and mortality, Berkman confirmed what some ancient peoples already knew well, making banishment their most severe punishment, a punishment feared far more than death.

Berkman continued her research to show the various problems that a lack of social supports poses to individual health and longevity. She found that social support must be of a certain quality to be effective. As she put it, "For social support to be health promoting, it must provide both a sense of belonging and intimacy and must help people to be more competent and self-efficacious."[3]

The appeal of vitamin connect *should* be unmatched because it costs nothing, can never be depleted, and does more to improve life than any other single force. But people walk right past it, barely even noticing it, as if it were a beer bottle in the gutter. While the average person may trivialize the power of this vitamin C, smart organizations understand it. The software firm SAS, for example, urges employees to bring their spouse and kids to join them at work for lunch. The Atlanta, Georgia, housing authority lowered the partitions between cubicles so people could see each other, which led to a major uptick in productivity and morale. The Harvard chemistry department saw a marked reduction in depression and suicide when it took steps to create a more connected culture.[4]

As I mentioned earlier, we live in a modern paradox of hyper-connection electronically, yet relative disconnection interpersonally. In their book *Connected,* Nicholas Christakis and James Fowler report on their study of three thousand randomly selected Americans. They set out to discover how many close social contacts people have, defining close social contacts as those people one discusses important matters with or spends free time with. They found that "the average American has just four close social contacts, with most having between two and six. Sadly, 12 percent of Americans listed no one . . . At the other extreme, 5 percent of Americans had eight such people."[5]

Christakis and Fowler go on to explain some of the compelling and surprising findings emerging from the study of social networks. For example, one of the qualities of social networks is contagion, the tendency for various moods, habits, and practices to flow through groups of people and affect not just those who know each other, but even friends of friends of friends. After three degrees of influence, as the authors put it, the effect drops off, but most of us are quite unaware that what our friends' friends' friends feel, think, and do affects us in a significant way. "This simple tendency for one person to influence another has tremendous consequences when we look beyond our immediate connections."[6]

So, not only is it good for you to connect, but also to choose your friends wisely, knowing of course that you can't control whom your friends or your friends' friends may befriend. Since "social networks . . . tend to magnify whatever they are seeded with," be it joy and optimism or obesity, depression, and violence, it is good to know as much as you can about the people you hang out with.[7]

The fact that positive energy is contagious and smiles are good for us has now been proven. Christakis and Fowler cite a study showing that when waiters were trained to offer "service with a smile, their customers report feeling more satisfied, and they leave better tips."[8] Not only that, based on a study of thirty-three male professional cricket players fitted with computers that recorded their moods during a match, "there was a strong association between a player's own happiness and the happiness of his teammates, independent of the state of the game; further, when a player's teammates were happier, the team's performance improved."[9]

The science is conclusive. The practical question becomes, how can a person live a connected life? The good news is that it's quite simple, as long as you take it seriously. To give you an idea of how to do that, here's a practical ten-step plan outlining how you could get your daily dose of this amazing "supplement," vitamin connect.

- SHARE A MEAL. Eat breakfast, dinner, or a midnight snack with someone every day. If you live alone, eat lunch with someone. Make a habit of having human moments, moments of in-person connection, rather than just electronic moments, throughout your day.

- MAKE TIME FOR MAKING LOVE. The most common sexual complaint I hear in my practice is that people don't make time for sex. If you have a partner, make time for sex. Sex is good for you in every measurable way, and every immeasurable way as well. It is impossible to be depressed, cynical, sad, upset, or in any other way less than fully alive while you're having an orgasm. Have many.

- KEEP PHOTOGRAPHS of people, pets, and places you love in your wallet or purse, and, if possible, in and around your work site. Look at them frequently.

- NEVER WORRY ALONE, at least not for an extended period of time. When you get worried for more than a little while, call someone, meet someone for coffee, or go to someone else's office. Pick the logical person to worry with, given the topic that's on your mind. When you worry alone, your worry quickly turns toxic. You become frozen in fear and your IQ plummets. When you connect with another person, you immediately feel less vulnerable and more powerful, even though the situation you're worried about hasn't changed at all. However, your ability to deal with it skillfully has skyrocketed.

- GO OUTDOORS, at least once a day, in addition to your commute. Commune, as they used to say, with nature. Drink nature in. Gaze up at the sky and let awe fill you. A blue sky with a cloud or two and sunshine is even better than gin with vermouth and a twist. Allow your mind to absorb the miraculous mental nutrients that radiate from nature, free of charge, albeit highly charged.

- OWN A PET. Pets are grand masters at providing vitamin connect. If you can't own a pet, try to associate with animals in any way you can. Most animals have solved the riddle of life, and they are eager to show you what they know. Let them. Freud himself owned a dog, a chow chow named Jofi, whom he adored. He kept her in the consulting room during his psychoanalytic sessions because he believed she calmed his patients.

- DEVELOP A BEST FRIEND AT WORK. Cultivate this relationship as much as you can, even if it cuts into your work time. Over time, the force of that friendship will more than pay for itself in increased productivity and desire to come to work. Having a best friend at work gives you something to look forward to on Monday morning. No matter how badly work may be going, such a friendship gives you someone to worry with, as well as someone with whom to have fun and celebrate success.

- OPT OUT OF OFFICE POLITICS. As delicious and seductive as they can be, resist indulging in the tantalizing treats of gossip, backbiting, and office politics as much as you possibly can. Often marvelously fun and engrossing in the moment, they turn work sour over time and inevitably exert a disconnecting influence on the culture you work in.

- MAKE TIME FOR FRIENDS AND FAMILY AWAY FROM WORK. And please, do it now, before it's too late. As a psychiatrist, one of the most painful laments I hear, and I hear it often, is, "Why didn't I do it when I could?" The gravest and most common mistake a dedicated worker makes is to set too low a priority on what he or she does away from work, especially with friends and family. You can't keep up close ties with all your friends, and you can't devote infinite time to your family, but you *can* commit enough time to keep those connections sufficiently lively that you look forward to them as the revitalizing reward in your life they ought to be.

- JOIN AN ORGANIZATION OUTSIDE OF WORK from which you derive great satisfaction and to which you make a valuable contribution. It may be a dinner club or a basketball or soccer team or an acting company. It may be a church, synagogue, or other religious group. It may be a chorus, a book group, an equestrian club, or a political group. Just find some organization that means a lot to you, that you derive fun from, and that you believe in enough to make time for.

Although vitamin connect is all-around wonderful, I offer a few important caveats.

As much as connection is such a force for good, it can also be destructive. Just look at the intense connections within gangs, or Mao's communist party, the Nazis in World War II, or the followers of Osama bin Laden. So deep and strong is the human need to connect, if a person does not find it in a healthy form, he will find it in a dangerous, sometimes evil form. While readers of this book are not going to join gangs or become terrorists, *we all must be careful of whom we choose to trust. While*

I advise people never to worry alone, I also advise them to choose with care the person they worry with.

I am a trusting person, too trusting in fact. I've been hurt by putting my trust in someone I took to be an ally, even a dear friend, only to have that person viciously stab me in the back. The instance I am referring to occurred in my business life, so I chalk it up to the cost of doing business. Nonetheless, it hurt me deeply and still causes me considerable distress when I think of it.

Still, when you find the right person to worry with, that person can become a godsend. My best friend, Peter Metz, is my go-to guy. We've been playing squash together on Tuesdays for thirty years. After our games, we go out for a drink and share our concerns as well as our joys. Those times with Peter save my life over and over.

Frame your problem so your friend can help you. Think of Les, the man with the electronics addiction. Let's say he goes to have a conversation with his friend, Joe, and says, "I really need help with what's become my internet addiction. I have a real problem. Can I talk to you about it?" Just the act of talking about it, exploring it, and letting the other person listen and react provides major assistance. Les could say, "I don't want or expect you to give me solutions. Please just listen and help me ask questions. Don't think that I'm burdening you with solving my problem. I just want you to listen and react."

This gives the other person permission to do the same thing with you, so you can help each other and deepen your connection. It's a process you don't have total control over but must trust. When you do it, a lot gets going in your unconscious. Solutions and new behaviors will emerge as if out of nowhere.

As I've said, you should create your own set of steps, your own action plan to fill your life with vitamin connect. Among the sensational six, this step is the most rewarding and the easiest to implement, and will surprise you the most with its extraordinary benefits. Our greatest joy and satisfaction lie in achievement and in intimacy, in work, and in love. Try to focus on both and not let one take over your life. Nothing beats it.

In addition to vitamin connect, there is another important thing that can improve your psychological health. I have a friend whose father had eleven heart attacks over ten years and died at the age of sixty-two. He was a hard-driving man who drank too much and suffered greatly in his life, which took a toll on his health. In the end, his heart was only about as strong as a rabbit's. He had difficulty getting out of bed in the morning, putting on his clothes, and going out to the hammock on the patio, where he spent his day lying under an orange tree, looking at the blossoms, smelling them, and gazing at the blue sky filtered through the shiny leaves. He was grateful for that, because in the end that's all he had. When I told my friend about vitamin connect, she said, "You ought to add to that vitamin G, which is gratitude."

There is solid empirical validation for my friend's placement of such a high value on vitamin G. In George Vaillant's longitudinal studies of which factors make for the most successful adaptations to life, gratitude ranks right at the top.[10] It doesn't matter that much what your lot in life is, but rather how you feel about your lot in life, an opinion you can control perhaps more than you realize. Or, as a rabbi once put it, "Happiness is not having what you want, but wanting what you have."[11]

field work: energy management through the day

If you've done the prep work and made full use of the sensational six practices, then the daily maintenance of energy will be far easier for you. But you can't expect your energy supply to be constant throughout the day. Therefore, it makes sense to find your own individual rhythm. When do you feel most energetic, most able to do difficult work? And when do you typically feel dull? Some people attend better with music playing, while walking around, or with someone else sitting in the room. Some people focus better in the morning, at night, in warm rooms, or in cold. Some need caffeine, others a hot shower. Some people focus in quick bursts, while others do their best working for long stretches, then resting for a day or even two. One size does not fit all; simply try to notice what works best for you.

Plan accordingly. *Don't shoot your wad. Conserve your best energy for your most significant work.* I'm at my best, for example, when I first arrive at work. It's what I call my "morning burst." Many people are like me. If you are, then be careful not to waste your morning burst by getting buried in e-mail. E-mail is a time suck. Unless there is something urgent that you absolutely must attend to, don't waste your precious energy. You don't want your morning burst to turn into your morning bust. Save your energy for the most demanding, most important tasks of the day. But try to operate within your basic patterns, your basic rhythms, rather than fighting them and always trying to modulate them.

Not only is it important to monitor your use of energy throughout the day, but also throughout the week, the month, the year. In this way, you can anticipate when you will work hard, and your mind and body can prepare for that, while you can also subconsciously know when you will not need to be "on."

harnessing the power of emotion

At the Phillips Exeter Academy in New Hampshire, where I went to high school, there was a legendary wrestling coach named Ted Seabrooke. He influenced thousands of students—most notably the novelist John Irving—through his coaching and his example. One of his memorable coaching axioms was, "Where the head goes, the body must follow."

I adapt Seabrooke's axiom here and say, "Where the heart goes, effort follows." We work hardest for what we care about most. People will work sixteen-hour days at jobs they hate in order to make money for what they love: their family. Emotion motivates us like nothing else.

Too often, people assume they can—or should—operate at their best no matter what kind of mood they're in. If we were all like *Star Trek*'s Mr. Spock, then mood would not matter. But since none of us is Vulcan, mood matters, far more than most people take into account. From school through every job we ever have, one of the most discriminating factors dictating our performance is how we feel while we are doing what we do.

Emotion impeded the progress of the characters we met in part I. Les tried to escape the emotions of everyday life through his blitzed-out screen sucking. Jean grew angry and impatient at feeling that she was being taken advantage of, which in turn retarded her efforts. Ashley's inability to focus on one thing led her to become frustrated with herself; her husband was close to the end of his rope as well. The combination of their frustrations reduced her ability to do anything well. Jack became a slave to his worrying. Mary cared so deeply about everyone else that she lost her ability to care for herself and her family. And Sharon lived in a state of ongoing negative emotion because she felt that she was under-achieving, which led her to underachieve all the more.

Positive emotion is key to peak performance. Extreme fear sharpens focus in the short term, but it subsides out of physiological necessity. Fear can't last long before it turns to something else: fatigue, numbness, or awareness of the danger without emotion attached. The supply of neu-rotransmitters, the electricity if you will, required to sustain extreme fear simply runs out after a short while.

Of course, fear remains a part of everyday life. At its best, it serves as a warning signal. But at its worst, it gets in the way and causes us to self-sabotage. As my old friend, the late, great learning specialist Priscilla Vail, said to me many times, "Emotion is the on/off switch for learning." If you are angry, anxious, or otherwise upset, the negative emotions short-circuit your focus on whatever you are doing. You focus more on how bad you feel or what's making you feel bad than on the work you want to do.

As Mary discovered, toxic emotion makes focus impossible. You can't compose a symphony, say, and carry on an argument simultaneously. Either you work on your symphony or you fight your fight, but you can't do both at once. If you are focusing on a spreadsheet and a colleague walks up to you with a Magnum and says, "I am going to blow your brains out because you stole my best idea, you rat bastard," you will not be able to continue to work on your spreadsheet. It's physically impossible. Even if you disarmed your irate colleague and sent him off handcuffed in the custody of the police, you would be so shaken that it would be hours, if not days, weeks, months, or even years, before you'd be able to concentrate fully on any spreadsheet again.

On the other hand, if you were working on that same spreadsheet and the same colleague came up to you and said, "Thanks for that nod of the head you gave me in the meeting yesterday. You have no idea how much I needed that," you'd feel renewed energy and focus, having just been given a dose of vitamin connect. This is because, in the brain, emotion rules. Deep within the brain are primitive centers that control the rest of the cerebrum. They've been in control for millions of years. These centers were elected to run the show in the brain early in evolution because they could protect us from danger far better than the fancy centers higher up in the cortex.

When these deep centers were jockeying for control, the cortex didn't even exist, let alone make its way to the top. Nature, no fickle force, still retains its power in the deep centers, where primitive emotions can prevail over reason and hijack the mind, making it impossible to concentrate on anything but the toxic emotions. Negative emotions like fear, anger, depression, the desire for revenge, or feeling wronged shanghai the mind and cause us to do stupid things, say things we regret later, and alienate people who would otherwise be helpful to us.

Not only does emotion influence focus and performance, it also affects health. However, the link isn't simple. We were once told that the type A personalities (the hard-driving competitive person, usually male) are at greater risk for heart attacks than the calmer type B's. But that conclusion collapsed when studied closely. Then we courted the type C personality, who was supposedly at greater risk for cancer. That notion perished under scrutiny as well.

Now we have type D. For the past twenty years, Dr. Johan Denollet and his team in the Netherlands have studied adults who score high on negative affect and social inhibition. Denollet calls them type D, for "distressed." His research correlates having type D personality with greater risk of heart disease and slower recovery time.[1] If you'd like to assess yourself (and who doesn't? We all love self-assessment quizzes), visit www.health.harvard.edu/newsweek/Type_D_for_distressed.htm.

If you're a type D personality—if you are chronically distressed—your risk of heart attack increases and your recovery time slows. It also means that you have greater trouble focusing than the average person, and you are more likely to self-sabotage.

Fortunately, there are many constructive steps you can take to tackle the problem. Pretty much every piece of advice in this book aims to reduce distress in your life so that you can perform at your best, so if you follow the tips throughout the book and retake the test in a month or two, your score will likely have changed.

a few mental tricks to clear your mind

The old days of the tyrannical boss or sadistic teacher are fast coming to an end, not because being a tyrant or a sadist is cruel or politically incorrect, but because tyrants and sadists fail. They don't get the best out of their people (or themselves, for that matter). Unhappy people underperform, while people who love what they're doing surpass their personal best all the time. If your mind is clear of negative emotions, then you are able to focus on the work without distraction. See the sidebar "Quick Tips for Managing Personal Psychology."

Since negative emotion can shatter focus, and does so frequently, look at yourself and consider for a moment that you may be misinterpreting a given situation. A little self-awareness could go a long way to help you clear yourself of clouds of negative feelings and beliefs.

We often create problems for ourselves and misinterpret reality by using psychological defense mechanisms that do not serve us well. Projection is common, so beware of it. In projection, you attribute to another person the feelings and beliefs you yourself hold.

QUICK TIPS FOR MANAGING
PERSONAL PSYCHOLOGY

As I've stated, while technology has spawned one part of the problem, a person's individual psychology makes a major contribution as well. Part of learning to manage modern life depends on learning to manage our own emotions and hang-ups. Nothing distracts a person more than being in emotional distress.

To help you get a handle on that part of the picture, your personal psychology, here are some quick tips to help you manage your own psyche better:

1. Work *with* your emotional grain, not against it. For example, if you like groups, work in groups and avoid being alone too much. On the other hand, if you like privacy and solitude, create structures that allow you to work on your own and not in groups too much. If you like to take chances, take chances; but if you don't, don't. If you get upset in the presence of conflict, be a peacemaker. On the other hand, if you like to fight, work in an arena where that's an asset, such as in certain kinds of law or entrepreneurism. It's the most revered and most time tested of all wisdom, put in different ways by the ancient Greeks, the Bible, the Torah, and Shakespeare: first *know yourself,* then *be true to yourself.*

2. Try to identify your hot buttons. What particularly annoys you? Is it a know-it-all? Is it someone who interrupts? Is it someone who won't ever say please or thank you? Is it someone who is obsequious? Someone who kisses up? Someone who's so PC she or he is a hypocrite? Is it a name dropper? A blowhard? A pedant? Try to name the hot buttons you know in advance will set you off more than they set off most people. Then when you see one coming, either get out of the way (i.e., leave the area) or suck it up and say to yourself, "I am not going to let this *$%@!# put me in a bad mood and ruin my workday. I am going to control my response and control the craziness within me that this person triggers."

3. Play armchair psychologist with yourself. Look back into your childhood, asking, "What issues came up then that carry through to today?" These issues are usually obvious. However, they may not be obvious to you, because we don't like to see painful matters, even if they are clear to everyone else. So, let someone you trust and who knows you well walk you through it. Are you a workaholic because your father was and you want to please him or outdo him? Are you insecure because you never got the unconditional love you needed early on? Are you ruthlessly competitive because you felt you always had to do it on your own? Are you unable to trust anyone because one of your parents betrayed you in a fundamental way? Were you the one who had to take care of your siblings because your parents, for whatever reasons, couldn't, and now you can't give up the habit of taking care of everyone? If you can identify these big, obvious issues, you can use insight and practice to overrule them. You can cease repeating the same mistake over and over, and in so doing, radically improve your focus on what matters most. Childhood issues can shanghai focus 24/7. A little insight can go a long way to empowering you to overrule those tendencies and hang-ups that are rooted in the past.

4. Know what turns you on. I don't mean sexually—of course, it's good to know that for other contexts. I mean what turns you on work-wise. What do you *love* to do? For a surgeon, it's performing surgery. For an entrepreneur, it's making a deal that turns a big profit. For a teacher, it's helping a struggling student suddenly understand. For a writer, it's writing a good sentence. Just as emotion can turn off peak performance, it can also turn it on. Know what turns you on. Then do that as much as you can.

5. Seek and accept help. Consider that someone else might know something you don't and may have insight that you could value.

The people who make the biggest messes of their lives—and in my line of work, I get to see many messes—are the people who refuse to listen to anyone else, who say it's my way or the highway, and who romance their own point of view to the point of choosing to fail rather than succeed by trying someone else's way. It's one thing to march to the beat of your own drummer, but quite another to block out all other instruments. Another piece of the foundational wisdom of Western culture—"Pride goeth before destruction, and a haughty spirit before a fall"—is just one of its best-known expressions.* It underpins almost every tragedy ever written, from the Greeks to Shakespeare to Herman Melville and Arthur Miller. Far worse than being a distraction, stubborn pride totally blinds a person.

*Proverbs 16:18, King James Version.

Projection is what drives paranoia. The paranoid person feels that people are out to get her because she is projecting her own aggressive feelings onto other people. Actually, they are not out to get her, *she is out to get them*, but she can't tolerate owning that feeling. She disowns it by projecting it onto others and wildly misreading reality.

Paranoia is common in everyday life. The extreme version, the violent, psychotic paranoid person, is rare. But most people lapse into moments of paranoia now and then. It is good to catch yourself, before you make stupid decisions based on projection.

Furthermore, paranoid feelings are hugely distracting and can preoccupy you all day, all week, sometimes all year. The ability to test your reality and snap out of a paranoid position can be a godsend.

Another common defense mechanism that gets us into trouble is denial. Also a primitive defense, like projection, denial leads us not to see what's right in front of us. We deny it, usually, because we don't know how to deal with it. Of course, by denying a problem, we only allow it to worsen. Like projection, denial is also common. A good guard against it is to invite people to tell you your foibles, insist that others speak up when they see something you don't, and never punish anyone for being honest with you, no matter how much you may not like to hear what they have to say.

A third common defense mechanism that can get you into trouble is reaction formation, which I discussed in relation to toxic handlers like Mary in chapter 5. When using reaction formation, you express the opposite of what you actually (unconsciously) feel. This explains why many people behave in a way opposite to their best interests: why they stay with a bad job or bad boss; why they accept substandard pay; why they allow others to take credit for work they've done; or why they accept abuse without protest.

Such people have enormous trouble acknowledging anger, sticking up for themselves, or being what they feel is selfish. Unlike the paranoid person, who projects his anger, the person using reaction formation turns the feeling into its opposite before it reaches consciousness.

The best way to deal with this is to ask yourself, "Why do I put up with this?" or listen when a caring colleague asks you the same question. When you get feedback from others that you are getting a raw deal, try not to play the martyr, as if that were somehow noble, but instead have a talk with yourself—or someone else—to get in touch with sane and useful feelings of aggression and self-assertion.

As I've stated throughout this book, the art of sustaining focus depends on many tricks, not the least of which is understanding yourself psychologically, and knowing where your blind spots might be. Shakespeare's King Lear lost his focus on how much his daughter, Cordelia, truly loved him because he fell prey to his desire to be loved and worshipped beyond possibility. Cordelia's sisters gave their father the insincere flattering words he craved. When Cordelia spoke the truth, that she loved him but would not sully that love in an insincere trumpeting of it, Lear banished her and set in motion his tragic downfall, as well as hers.

Lear lost focus on that most important of all objects of focus—the truth—because his insatiable need to be worshipped blinded him to the true love his daughter felt for him.

How many bosses do you know like that? How many have you worked for? It seems the more power a person acquires, the less able he or she becomes to hear hard truths. How many managers fail to grow as much as they could because they can't handle the truth, to quote the famous line from *A Few Good Men*?[2]

Staying focused requires an ability to handle the truth. Handling the truth requires an ability to know your weak spots, psychologically. If, for example, Lear had been able to say, "As I grow older and closer to death, I feel a growing need for love and reassurance, to give me the courage to face the end of my reign and of my life," then he would have avoided losing everything, including the daughter who loved him most.

c-state versus f-state

The sensational six practices will go a long way toward helping you balance your emotions, but there are times when you will still feel spent, tired, foggy, or irritable. You will find yourself moving from what I call C-state—cool, calm, collected, careful, curious, courteous, caring, consistent, concentrated—into what I call F-state—fearful, fatigued, feeble, frantic, forgetful, frustrated, feckless, fractious, flakey, and about to utter another f-word.

You should have a file in your mind of instant interventions, because if you stay in F-state for long, you can do a ton of damage to your work and to yourself. In F-state, people sabotage their good work. As you feel your energy draining, and you feel F-state creeping in, try any one of the following:

- HAVE A HEALTHY SNACK. Fruit, veggies, hummus, nuts, a piece of dark chocolate.

- DO A QUICK BURST OF EXERCISE. Take what Dr. John Ratey calls a "brain break"—twenty-five fast jumping jacks, ten quick push-ups, and a one-minute burst of rapid running in place will instantly reset your brain. If you can't do that, try walking up and down stairs as fast as you can for two minutes. If you can't do that, go for a brisk walk through the building or, even better, outdoors.

- MEDITATE OR TAKE A POWER NAP. Just five minutes of meditation will revive you and, when you see your thoughts floating by without attaching emotion to them, you gain a positive objectivity. If you are really tired, take a power nap. But beware, some people can't do this; they end up either wasting time or falling asleep for too long. If you can do it, though, set the alarm on your cellphone for fifteen or twenty minutes, and go to sleep. When it works, it does wonders.

- ENJOY A DOSE OF VITAMIN CONNECT. Call a friend, chat with a colleague about something fun, listen to a favorite piece of music (yes, you can get vitamin connect from inanimate sources like music, art, photos, poetry, essays, even memories).

- USE DRUGS. I'm being a bit facetious here, but caffeine can provide a burst of energy. Just don't use it as your mainstay. And, if you have ADHD, this may be the signal to take your next dose of Ritalin, Adderall, or whatever your doctor has prescribed. (See the appendix for a discussion of stimulants and other medications.)

- USE HUMOR. Laughter revives the mind wondrously well. Keep a joke book in your desk drawer. Or go to YouTube and find something funny to look at.

- EXPERIMENT. Come up with remedies that work best for you. As long as they are safe and legal, anything goes.

beating unhappiness at work

Lining up your goals with your emotions and your emotions with your goals is critical. Otherwise, you will be stripping your gears throughout your life. You will never be able fully to focus on your goal and pursue it with a passion if your heart's not in it.

Many years ago, Andrew Carnegie commissioned Napoleon Hill to interview five hundred of the wealthiest, most successful individuals at the time, including Henry Ford, John D. Rockefeller, George Eastman, F. W. Woolworth, and Thomas Edison. The goal of the project was to determine what factors led to great success. Hill's 1937 book, *Think and Grow Rich*, is now one of the classics in the genre of self-help and has sold many millions of copies. The number-one quality, the "secret" he touts in the introduction that can be found "on every page" and in the life of every person he interviewed, is "a burning desire" to succeed. Call it "the fire in the belly," "a calling," "the will to succeed," "a work ethic," whatever, you will not find great success without this intense desire, this intense emotion.

Think about the way many great generals put a lot of thought into getting their troops ready for battle. Why do you think we have military music? It's not sophisticated music (someone, either Groucho Marx or George Clémenceau, I can't find a definitive source, once famously remarked, "Military justice is to justice as military music is to music"), but military music gets the job done. It pumps soldiers up and engages their emotions. So it is in the battle to achieve your goals. Without a fire in the belly, your efforts lack luster.

find and work within your sweet spot

If we were machines, then we wouldn't need to worry about the emotions that criticism might stir up, because there would be no emotion to stir up.

Some might protest, "What do you mean? We employ adults. They are professionals. The paycheck should be all the praise they need. They should be able to take criticism, say thank you very much, benefit from it, make the recommended changes, and move on."

Show me one person who is truly that professional. I suppose you might be able to find one, if you looked long enough, but most of the time you'll find people who pretend to be like that, then go home and mutter into their Scotch about what a rotten place they work at.

If you play golf (as I do, poorly), you've heard the phrase, "It will keep you coming back," referring to the effect of one good shot. When you do something well that's difficult to do, that's about as much fun as a person can have, at work anyway. No matter how many bad shots you hit and all the misery they caused you, that one good shot was so much fun it keeps you coming back for more.

Finding the fun, at least at work, means to me finding that one good shot I make each day. Maybe two, maybe three or more. But, usually I make at least one. I try to hold on to that as I drive home. I try not to make the mistake of many people by reviewing each and every bad shot as they drive home. (By doing that, you gradually condition yourself to hate your job.)

Who wants to go to a place of failure day in and day out? The old adage about learning from your mistakes is true enough, but new evidence suggests we actually improve more by dwelling on our successes than by reviewing mistakes. This is because the more you can associate work with success, the more you're going to want to go to work, and the more, ironically, you're going to be open to learning from your mistakes. Positive emotion allows you to focus better on what's difficult, while negative emotion leads you, over time, to use avoidance as a coping style.

There is a subtle distinction here. Taken to the extreme, neither position works well. If you never look at a mistake and learn from it, you will endlessly repeat mistakes. On the other hand, if you never relish success and spend all your time dwelling on what you've done wrong, you will soon get depressed or simply become grim.

I suggest only that you lean more toward relishing the good shots, however few they may be, than dissecting what you did poorly. Most people are not very good self-examiners anyway, so the effort to look at what went wrong is fraught with self-deception. But should another person whom you trust and know has your best interests at heart point out a mistake you've made, take it seriously. That person is doing you a favor, because he or she has a vantage point you can never have.

Do yourself a favor: rather than telling yourself to work harder, invoking the famous work ethic so many people rightly extol, it makes much better sense to put yourself in a position where your hardest work will naturally follow, without commands from above, without a strong work ethic, in fact without any ethic at all. You will work your hardest *because you want to.* The work *ethic* becomes a *passion for your work,* a love for what you do, whatever you do. I call this working in your sweet spot. You can find your sweet spot by looking to see where three spheres intersect, as shown in figure 11-1.

The first sphere comprises all that you love to do. The second sphere comprises all that you have significant talent at doing. The third sphere comprises all that advances the mission you're on, or, put differently, all that someone will pay you to do. The intersection of these three spheres is the magical realm I call your sweet spot.

The more time you spend in your sweet spot, the happier and more successful you'll be, the more likely you'll be in flexible focus or flow, and the more motivated to work hard you'll feel. On the other hand, the more time you spend outside your sweet spot, the more frustrated and deprived you'll feel, the more in F-state and the less successful you will be.

So let's say you are unhappy at work. You feel that you aren't using your talent or brains or training to their highest capacity, and you don't feel challenged. Do you simply draw a paycheck day after day, or do you try to do something about it? Sadly, most people see no alternative but to

FIGURE 11-1

Working in your sweet spot

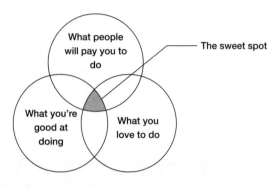

accept their unhappiness. They fear that if they bring up their unhappiness to their supervisors, they will fall under suspicion or perhaps even lose their jobs. There is an even more unfortunate side effect to this attitude; if you are unhappy at work, it will spill out in one form or another and very often in the form of self-sabotage. You may do your work poorly; you may come in late and leave early; you may do as Les did and waste time surfing the net. There are a million ways to ruin your professional career by not doing the most critical work of managing yourself.

As a psychiatrist, I can tell you that the clients and patients I've worked with have been pleasantly surprised when they have an honest conversation with their supervisors. For example, once Les went through a course of therapy to break his internet addiction, he realized that he had been unhappy at work. So he went to his supervisor and said, "I'd like to have a conversation about how I'm being utilized at this company." He'd come to this conversation having done his homework; he had already located another position in the company that he thought would be a better fit for him.

This honest conversation was helpful in several ways. Les was encouraged to apply for another, lateral position in the firm in marketing, where he could use more of his creative skills and where he flourished.

His supervisor was able to hire someone who was quite happy and successful in Les's old job. And Les went from being internet addicted, distracted, and disgruntled to sane, happy, and, well, "gruntled." (If you are a manager, don't wait to have these kinds of honest conversations with employees, who may be reluctant to take the first step. Obviously, it's in everyone's best interest to have the right people with the right skills in the right positions, much more efficient to move someone than to fire him and then rehire and train someone else.)

In managing your emotional life, try to set your default position to "life is good." The Roman Stoic philosopher Epictetus embodied the often-ignored power of doing this. He was a crippled slave. Despite being beaten frequently, despite being crippled, and despite being owned by another person, he was happy. His master was so impressed that he told Epictetus he would free him if he could teach him how to be happy. Epictetus told his master that the one thing a person can control is his opinions. As he advised, "Do not seek to have events happen as you want them to, but instead want them to happen as they do happen, and your life will go well."[3] Despite the wretched external circumstances of his life, Epictetus determined to hold the opinion that life was good, and to feel grateful for the chance to be alive. His master was so impressed that he freed Epictetus, who spent the rest of his life teaching others his philosophy. One of his students, Flavius Arrianus, compiled his sayings into a small book, *The Enchiridion* (The Handbook), which Roman soldiers found so inspiring they often read them just before marching into battle.[4]

By setting your default position at "life is good," you prime yourself not to fall into the swamps of negative emotion that surround life. Many sophisticated intellectuals scoff at this idea, deeming it simplistic if not silly. Yet, it has ancient and sturdy intellectual roots, as embodied in the life and work of the great Stoic philosopher.

Negative feelings cloud focus and reduce your vim. So try to turn down the volume of the part of you that disagrees, that thinks life is lousy. How you feel, your emotional state, often creates the content of your thinking. Emotion can precede and indeed create the content of your thoughts. We usually assume that content—what's going on inside and outside our minds—creates emotion. But it can be just the opposite. What you feel can create what you think and what you do. The more you can be in a life-is-good frame of mind, the better you will do.

harnessing the power of structure

Sister Joan Chittister, a Benedictine nun, writer, and speaker, takes part in the training and supervision of new members of her order. Early in their training, she asks her eager novitiates a basic question: "Why do we pray?" One new nun will raise her hand and say, "Because we love the Lord and wish to worship Him every day."

"That's true," Sister Joan will reply, "but that's not why we pray."

Perplexed and naive, another earnest young nun will raise her hand and propose, "We pray because we want to strengthen our spiritual connection with God."

"Yes," Sister Joan will reply, "but that's not why we pray."

By now the nuns are feeling frustrated, as they believe they know perfectly well why they pray, and they wonder what other reason the revered Sister Joan could possibly have in mind.

Another ardent nun summons up her courage and takes a stab at the question. "We pray," she pronounces, "to draw closer to Jesus and to quiet our troubled souls. We pray to lift our hearts and minds from worldly worries to the spiritual world. We pray to express gratitude and seek forgiveness."

"That's all true," Sister Joan replies, "but that's not really why we pray."

Yet another nun, hoping to be the one finally to get the right answer, raises her hand. "We pray because we're supposed to pray," she volunteers.

Sister Joan smiles. "That's close," she says. "But that's not quite why we pray." She pauses, sensing the frustration in the room. What possible answer could she be looking for, all the frowning faces seem to be asking.

"We pray," Sister Joan finally states, "because the bell rings."

Each day, no matter what their mood or what their circumstances, the nuns all gather for worship when the bell rings. In the most practical and superficial sense, they gather *because* the bell rings. In the most fundamental of ways, they pray if for no other reason than *it is simply what they do after the bell rings*. That bell offers a perfect example of structure.

why work to create structure?

Life depends upon structure. Throughout all of nature, we see magnificent examples of structures that allow for life. I've already described the constructal law and how it governs all movement, the very definition of life. But creating structure is difficult because it goes against a basic law of physics.

When we think, we are trying to make order out of chaos. In doing so, we wrestle with the second law of thermodynamics, which states that nature tends toward a state of maximum disorder, or entropy. In thinking, as we work to bring order out of chaos, nature snaps at us, rebuffing our effort, and recoils. "Keep out," nature seems to say. "I have my secrets, and they are mine to keep."

But we mortals will not be put off. We must eat of the tree of knowledge. We persist in thinking, in trying to wrest order out of disorder, in trying to pry the secrets out of nature's hiding places. As exhausting and painful as it can be, we humans keep at it, eternally.

One reason we do it is to get paid. As Samuel Johnson said, "No man but a blockhead ever wrote except for money."[1] But why pick such a frustrating line of work, the work of the mind, when there are so many easier ways to get paid? People do it, Johnson most assuredly included, because when it goes right, it feels good, perhaps better than anything else ever feels. It feels good to win one skirmish with entropy, to defeat the devil of disarray, to hammer out order, to create beauty, to perceive a pattern in what seemed random, to turn a witty phrase, to nail a perfect landing off the high bar of thought, to create a moment's harmony in a cacophonous relationship, to design a machine that does what you ask it to do, to write a sentence that says what you want it to say. In short, it feels good to prevail against the forces of destruction, forces that will one day bring every life down, but for one wondrous, weightless moment, you defy.

Sometimes, rarely, a great idea actually jumps into your boat and you take it home. Oh, lucky day. But usually, you have to work, sometimes an entire lifetime, to land just one big one. If you are like Ashley, you get many bites—many new ideas hit your bait—but that is a far cry from reeling any one of them all the way in.

How many people have had hundreds of ideas for a new business? But how many people actually start one, let alone one that succeeds? How many people think of an invention they can't wait to patent? But how many people actually take their invention to the market? How many people have a great idea for a book, but how many actually write and publish the book? How many people believe they're just one hit away from the big score? But how many score big?

One moment you think you have a thought hooked, but then, with not so much as a fare-thee-well, it's gone. You're left wondering what happened, where it went, how it got away. Some of these "fish" have been hooked often before, only to have escaped many times. There they lie like fat, old trout, free, in a deep pool beneath a fallen tree, smugly looking up at you and me.

Our best hope, Ashley's best hope, is to invent the right net, the right structure to catch them. As Dan Sullivan, a renowned teacher of entrepreneurs, says, "The best ideas are caught, not taught."[2] Such is the power of structure that it can dictate, facilitate, and bring order to most everything we do. It is imperative in today's crazy-busy world to create structures that enable you to do what you want to do, and prevent you from doing what you do not want to do.

Some examples of structure: An appointment book. A closed door. An open door. A rhyme scheme. A switch in the "off" position. A day set aside to rest. Grammar. The opening bell. A list. A date night. Rhythm. An alarm clock. Laws. An egg timer next to your computer. Politeness. Equations. Biting your tongue. Seasons. The idea that "To every thing there is a season, and a time to every purpose under the heaven."

You must act and do. You have no choice. Every day, you act and do, until you can't. While you *can* ignore the sensational six practices and do nothing to get your brain ready for action, or do nothing to create the optimal emotional state in which to act, you *cannot* avoid taking action. All day, every day, you act. Your brain fires signals nonstop, day and night. Barring brain death, your brain is going to act whether you want it to or not until you die.

Structure is a simple-sounding but truly life-changing tool that allows you to plan and control in order to achieve your goals. A plan is itself an excellent example of structure. Without structure is chaos. Without structure, you get sidetracked. Without structure, you go off on tangents, hopping from one great opportunity to the next, but capitalizing on none of them. Emotion goes unchecked. Distractions and interruptions flood your world. Your thoughts and actions zigzag and vector like snowflakes in a snow squall, a flurry of activity that bursts upon the scene, then disappears just as quickly.

An invisible haze holds many people back. Their days lack direction and coherence, due to lack of structure. Each time they try to reach the next level of achievement, they fall back, as if blocked by the haze that they cannot see. The haze may be caused by disorganization, lack of focus, poorly defined goals, loss of energy, depression, overcommitment, lack of support, or a host of other obstacles. The way to penetrate the haze is to create structures that burn right through it.

With structure—with a plan, a schedule, a prioritization of your goals—you can put yourself in position to win, to do what your best self wants you to do. If you're a nun, you put yourself in a pew to pray because the bell rings and tells you to. If you're a trader on the stock exchange, you put yourself on the exchange floor and start making trades when that particular bell rings, because it allows you to.

Ironically, many creative people resist structure and thereby sabotage their best selves. Aspiring entrepreneurs like Ashley have said to me, "I can't be tied down to a routine or a flow chart. I need to have the freedom to do what I want, when I want. I'm too independent and creative to be tied down." To those people I say, "Good luck. Come back and see me when you're tired of underachieving." If they do come back, I say, "OK, now let's make friends with structure. Start by looking at arguably the two greatest creative geniuses who ever lived, Shakespeare and Mozart."

Take Shakespeare. Almost every play he wrote was in blank verse. Iambic pentameter. Da-DA, da-DA, da-DA, da-DA. "If music be the food of love . . ."—four iambs. But then comes, "play on"—a spondee, two stressed syllables. So Shakespeare was not a metronomic slave to iamb after iamb. But the form gave him the basic structure within which he could create endless variety. Without the form of blank verse, he would have had no boundaries to cross, no pattern to work against, and we would have a mess instead of the greatest, most majestic yet intricate beauty ever achieved in the English language, indeed in any language at all.

Mozart composed within tight musical forms that led to monotonous music in the hands of other composers, but in Mozart's hands, those forms led to boundless variety. Much of the beauty and excitement of his music derives from its element of surprise, but the surprise is only a surprise due to the expectation set by the structure Mozart was working within.

While his contemporaries—most notably, Antonio Salieri—composed good music, their scores lacked the transcendence and originality of Mozart. He drove his competitors into fits of envy. But Mozart would never have been able to make what he did of his genius had he not mastered the forms and structure within which he composed.

Far from being the killjoy many creative people fear structure to be, it is quite the opposite. It facilitates joy.

creating structure

The failure to use simple structures leads to ongoing underachievement. Usually it is not a lack of awareness that some structure, like a list, might help, but rather an inability to use a structure or tool you know will help. To tap the power of structure, take a specific problem or goal of yours and ask yourself, what sort of structure might help me solve this problem or achieve this goal? For example, let's say your goal is to get more exercise. This is a common goal, yet it is one that eludes most people. For every jogger you see running the roads, there are dozens who wish they were or are resolving so to do as they drive past.

The best way to make sure you get enough exercise is to schedule it. Schedule = Structure. Pick a time, say 7 a.m. on Monday, Wednesday, and Saturday and put it into your calendar. If you worry you might sleep in, schedule the exercise with someone, so you have to show up or let the other person down. If even that fails, then hire a trainer, so if you skip, you still have to pay for the session. This is a variation on Sister Joan's bell. You don't have to decide to go to the gym because the decision has been made in advance. It is what you do at the appointed time on the appointed day.

OUTLINE FOR SETTING GOALS

1. **Short term:** Set three goals per day. Only three. Having too many goals chokes progress. Once you achieve the three, if there's still time, you can set another, then another.

2. **Medium term:** Set three goals per two-week term.

3. **Long term:** Set three goals per six months to a year.

4. **Lifetime:** Define your lifetime goals. This list may exceed three items, but be careful not to make it too long. Of course, these may change at any time, but the exercise is worthwhile to define what you want to achieve before you die . . . before you die.

5. **Assess your progress regularly.** This improves focus and motivation, even if you are falling short.

6. **Review and revise.** Review your goals regularly. It is the best way to keep your mind fresh. You can revise these lists at any time. Write them down, as they have a way of morphing in your mind into forms you didn't intend. Even if you do not revise them, check on them periodically to make sure you are on track.

Setting goals in an organized fashion forces you to do one of the most difficult and important tasks in today's world: *prioritize.* The great achievement of modern life is also its curse: *you can do so much.* In order to turn that curse into a blessing, you must prioritize.

Clearly defined goals—short, medium, and long term, and lifetime—focus the mind marvelously.

You can actually put a lot of creativity into developing structure. For example, I once treated a woman who had a problem with impulsive overspending. She ran up large credit card debt, to the point where her financial adviser wanted her to get rid of all her credit cards. But she didn't want to give them up altogether, in case she really needed them. She came up with the following solution. She took the credit cards and put them into a bowl of water. She then put the bowl of water into the freezer. The credit cards would be there should she really need them, but they would be separated from her impulse to spend by a barrier of ice. That's genius-level structure.

A decision is an act of creating structure, like an on-off switch: "I will do this; I will not do that." People often try to wiggle out of this kind of structure, as it limits their freedom.

CrazyBusy app

To help people structure their days, I created an app called CrazyBusy, which you can download for free. It contains various features, including one that allows you to input variables that lead to the calculation of a "worth-it" factor of a given task to help you decide if you should do it. It also contains a stopwatch, tips on managing modern life, an assessment tool to let you visualize where you are actually spending your time (you'd be amazed at how most people are quite unaware of this), various brain games and focus exercises, and methods for preserving C-state (calm, concentrated, careful, creative) and avoiding F-state (frustrated, forgetful, frantic, feckless). The user-friendly app offers a simple, practical way to add structure to your day, getting more done that needs to get done, while avoiding the unimportant but time-consuming tasks and activities.

make it fun

A big reason people don't create the structures that could help them is that they believe it is tedious. It seems onerous. Boring. To take full advantage of the power of creating structures, it's best to make doing so *fun*.

As Steven Kotler wrote: "What's painfully ironic is that flow is a radical and alternative path to mastery *only* because we have decided that play—an activity fundamental to survival, tied to the greatest neurochemical rewards the brain can produce, and flat out necessary for achieving peak performance, creative brilliance, and overall life satisfaction—is a waste of time for adults. If we are hunting the highest version of ourselves, then we need to turn work into play and not the other way round. Unless we invert this equation, much of our capacity for intrinsic motivation starts to shut down. We lose touch with our passion and become less than what we could be."[3] Making a game out of structure can turn the humdrum into the appealing. It can also force a change in behavior.

For example, Volkswagen sponsored a contest in Germany to reduce the number of people who drove above the speed limit. The winner of the contest created a "speeding lottery," in which each car that passed a camera had its speed noted. If the car was speeding, the driver received a citation in the mail. But if the car was obeying the speed limit, that driver received a check drawn from the pool of money collected from the speeders. Once the speeding lottery was set up, the average speed at the site of the camera dropped from thirty-two kilometers per hour to twenty-five, a 21 percent reduction.[4]

In Sweden, a contest was held to encourage pedestrians to take the stairs, rather than the adjacent escalator, when coming up from a subway station. The winning entry turned the stairs into piano notes so that the person climbing the stairs created a musical tone with every step. Users of the stairs increased dramatically, up 66 percent.

In a park in Europe, a trash bin was rigged with a device that made the whining sound of a bomb being dropped, capped off with the sound of an explosion when a piece of trash was dropped into the bin. The responsive sound intrigued kids, who started looking for trash to throw away; adults did as well. The rigged bin took in seventy-two kilograms of trash in one day, compared to the normal bin across the park that only took in forty-one kilograms on the same day.

Another contest encouraged more people to recycle bottles by putting them into a sidewalk bottle bin. The winner of the contest came up with the idea of turning the bin into an arcade, so that when you put a bottle in, lights flashed, music played, and a score appeared on a screen. On the first evening, nearly a hundred people used the bottle bin arcade, while only two people used the normal bin across town. Just as turning a bottle bin into an arcade can help people do the otherwise dull task of bringing bottles to a recycling center, so can adding novelty to any drab task turn it into a task a person is more likely to perform. Like the innovators at thefuntheory.com, any of us can use imagination to turn drudgery into a task we will do rather than avoid.

practical solutions

Think of a specific problem or goal that you have. Then ask yourself, "How could a different structure help me?" The new structure you develop may be at the macro level, such as finding a different job or buying a new information storage system; or it may be at the micro level, such as moving a meeting to a time of day when you tend to focus better, or asking your assistant to deny interruptions during the 10 a.m. hour every Wednesday, so you can think. The key is to be creative and also to think big in terms of the powerful difference a new structure can make in your life.

Get well enough organized to do your work, but don't think your organization must be perfect. The best structures are the ones you invent yourself. Get into the habit of thinking in terms of external structure that can help you overcome internal obstacles.

Finally, remember: curtail, delegate, and eliminate (CDE). The more you can simplify your life, the more structural control you will gain. At first, CDE seems difficult. After all, everything is there for a reason, right? Wrong. Most of us have allowed clutter to fill not only our desks, closets, cars, and drawers, but also our schedules. Much as I touted the ringing of the bell as an excellent reason to pray or do anything, we also can become blind slaves to bells we neither set up nor desire. They become like car alarms going off in empty parking lots.

So, go through your life, both your physical spaces and schedules, wielding a scalpel ruthlessly, ready to cut all you can. Once you curtail, delegate, and eliminate, *leave the free space empty*, at least for a while. The law of the physics for modern life is that *you must take your time, or it will be taken from you.*

distracted no more

I work in the hope business. I work in a world of trying to help "if only's" come true. One of the rewards of my job is discovering that *no* situation is ever so dire that hope cannot spark within it, given the right fanning of the embers.

I've also learned that people, for the most part, do the best they can. They cobble together a life, sometimes turn it into a shambles, but even in the shambles, they are doing their best at that particular time. Few people *intend* to do less well than they can.

A great phrase that Joseph Wood Krutch attributes to Anatole France succinctly sums up what I have learned we all do: "*Chacun fait son salut comme il peut.* 'Every one seeks his salvation as he may' . . . [that phrase] expresses the idea . . . both of the comprehensive liberty there granted and of that sweeping refusal to make moral distinctions which is implied in the masterfully malicious adroitness with which the single word *salut* is made to include any desire which a man may have, from Augustine's thirst for God on down to the last perverse whim which has taken possession of the debauchee whose desires are, no doubt, just as imperious and as little to be questioned as are those of any one else."[1]

Each of the six characters I created for this book was doing the best he or she could at the time. Revisiting the six characters makes for a fitting conclusion to our journey into the world of attention deficit trait or ADT, personal focus, and individual psychology. Here's how each of the characters might have progressed.

Les suffered with an addiction. His addiction was the newest one, electronics. In helping Les to see that he was medicating himself (to use Edward Khantzian's term I cited in chapter 1) with his electronics, I was able to get him to address the larger matter: what disease, or dis-ease, was he trying to medicate? In his case, it was a low-grade depression born out of a fear that he didn't have the talent to live up to the expectations that his wife, his boss, and he himself had. Once he was able to modify his use of electronics, he became better able to work with Carl, his boss, and begin to unwrap his considerable gifts at work, which of course translated into progress at home as well.

Jean's effort to reclaim her life was not easy. As with all people, change comes slowly, haltingly, and with setbacks. However, when she did see and feel the shipwreck of her life, the idea that came to her was more of a command. *I've simply got to take back control*, she said to herself. *I can't let myself get pushed around.*

When insight actually helps and leads to change, it is usually not the novelty of the insight or its brilliance that helps, because most important insights regarding one's life are neither novel nor brilliant. Indeed, they are usually quite mundane because they've occurred to people millions of times before: Know yourself. Speak the truth. Follow your passion. Be true to who you are. Don't worship false idols. Focus on what matters most. Don't live your life for and through others. Understand that your boss is not your father or mother. Be real. Stick up for yourself. Realize you are no longer a child. Each of these commonplace insights can change a life dramatically for the better.

What gives an insight its power is the context in which it occurs, its timing. When Jean felt the pain of her circumstance in the extreme, saw her shipwreck, to use Ortega's term, then the ordinary insight, *I have more control than I am using*, took on great power. She used her new-found strength to take many of the steps I've recommended throughout, from cutting back on commitments to finding warm connections with friends to preserving time alone for meditation and standing up to her spouse. It was not easy. But desperation led her to change.

Ashley suffered with one of life's most crippling afflictions: a narcissistic parent, in her case, her mother. However, it need not ruin her life. As I've stated and have seen repeatedly, nothing need ruin a life. There is always, always hope. In one of our sessions, Ashley came up against how cruel her mother had been, how jealous and selfish. I sat with Ashley as she welled up. "This will never change, will it?" she asked me.

"What your mother did will never change. But what you feel and do can absolutely change."

"Really?" she asked. "Tell me the truth, damn it!"

"I'm telling you the truth. You can walk out of the desert your mother created."

At that moment, she dared to hope, where she had not dared before. Now, she had to practice hope. And she had to practice making decisions, adding structure to her life, eating and sleeping better, and making love more often. All these forces—the psychological, the practical, the physiological—combined to create the progress she made.

Jack was so wedded to worry that he lost the woman he wed. Worry was in his genes and in his early upbringing. To let go of toxic worry would require Jack to be willing to give up the very state of mind in which ironically he felt most safe. Medication made a big difference for Jack. At first, he was unwilling to take it, but when he saw how empty his life was becoming, when he saw the shipwreck, he decided something had to give. In prescribing Zoloft for him, I picked a serotonin reuptake inhibitor, because the neurotransmitter is key in regulating worry, anxiety, and mood. Medication gave Jack a jump start, but he needed more than just that. I prescribed vigorous daily physical exercise, perhaps the best medication of all for toxic worry, as well as hefty doses of vitamin connect. Jack and I met regularly for over a year. He used our sessions to reorient himself in the world of imagination, and test out life with less toxic worry. While he never freed himself of toxic worry altogether, he did become able to approach his wife and show her a different enough version of himself that the family reunited.

Mary's problem was that her focus on others had saved not only her but her entire family while she was growing up. To relinquish that habit would be to enter what she felt to be highly dangerous territory. But she was miserable as an adult, taking care of everyone but herself. I worked with her to help her understand that taking care of oneself is not selfish, in the negative meaning of that word, but selfish in the best sense. Only by taking care of oneself is one able to take care of others. In bearing with the tension of feeling selfish, Mary could see the shipwreck she'd created. In that state of despair, the idea that came to her was crude and simple: *Screw this!*

Anger flooded her. Good anger. Anger she'd pushed away for decades. She lived with that anger for months, and allowed it to guide away situations she used to plow right into—people and projects in distress.

I prescribed exercise, meditation, and a regular lunch with a friend. I urged Mary to talk to her friend about herself, not just about the friend, to learn how to do it. To her pleasure and amazement, the friend liked hearing about Mary, and noted how this was so different. She would backslide from time to time, but her fundamental insight, that she did not want to sacrifice her life to the pleasure of others nor did she need to for others to survive, put her on a track toward a better life.

Sharon's progress was most dramatic of all, because she had a treatable condition that usually responds quickly and powerfully to the interventions we are lucky enough to have. The lesson to be learned from Sharon is how important it is that the public understand not only ADHD but learning differences in general. From David Neeleman to Richard Branson to Charles Schwab, some of our most talented people have learning differences. We need start recognizing the enormous talents often embedded in learning differences.

As we come to the end of this journey into modern life and the common mistakes people make as they work to stay on track, let me offer a few summarizing suggestions on how to stay focused, boost productivity, and remain sane:

1. PRIORITIZE AND FOCUS on what matters most . . . this minute, this hour, this day, this week, this year, this decade, this lifetime.

2. RECOGNIZE THE UNMATCHED POWER OF LOVE and the human connection in everyday life.

3. DOWNLOAD THE CRAZYBUSY APP. Create boundaries that make it impossible for you to be pulled in too many directions at once. Remember the constructal law: remove obstacles to free flow.

4. RECOGNIZE THAT PLEASURE IS NOT THE SAME AS JOY, and that stimulation is not the same as substance.

5. ALLOW FOR DOWNTIME. Remember, when you are doing nothing, your brain and its default network are doing a lot.

6. PRESERVE THE HUMAN MOMENT. Don't allow the electronic moment to overrun your life.

7. LEARN TO TAKE CARE OF YOURSELF. Say no. Don't give everything away.

8. DON'T ASSUME THAT WORKING HARDER IS THE ANSWER. Most likely, working smarter is. This whole book has been about how to work smarter.

9. WORK AS MUCH AS POSSIBLE IN YOUR SWEET SPOT: the overlap of what you love to do, what you're good at doing, and what advances the mission or someone will pay you to do.

10. TRY TO FOLLOW THE BASIC PLAN: energy, emotion, engagement, structure, control.

cheerleading

I've offered a plan to master the magic of mental clarity, a plan that once understood leads you to see that mental clarity needs no magic at all, just science in action. I've suggested that in this era, we need to be more deliberate, even scientific, about creating and sustaining flexible focus than ever before because the thieves of our attention, even of our very minds, are cleverer and more predatory than anyone dreamed they could become.

We live in an utterly different world from that of even two decades ago, teeming with possibility, shining with hope in places, but shrouded in doubt and fear in others. It is a world that can take us over, if we're not careful. More control of our minds is up for grabs than it's ever been in history. Once a fine and private place, the mind is private no more.

Now it is critical to know how to own, manage, protect, and develop your mind according to your own desires, not someone else's, while not being sucked into the whirlpool of useless but seductive information, ideas, and rhetoric. By learning how to cultivate the state of mind I've named flexible focus, a state in which you can both come up with new ideas as well as develop them fully, you can take charge of modern life rather than letting it take charge of you. The stupefied screen sucker, so common now in the workplace, symbolizes the jeopardy this modern world flirts with every day.

But, just as we've never been so vulnerable to attack, we've never been as powerful. By taking charge and by learning the skill of regulating focus not only can improve your own mind and develop it according to your own desires, rather than someone else's, but you can also succeed far beyond what you imagined was possible. That's because never before has so much been possible.

Be creative. Be like the people who turned stairs into piano notes. Don't let your ideas melt like snowflakes on warm pavement. Catch them, preserve them, feed them, and systematically see to it that they grow.

- Court flow.

- Maintain your mental energy at its best.

- Follow the sensational six practices.

- Get into the right emotional space, created by working in your sweet spot.

- Build the structures that will allow you to achieve in ways that will satisfy you beyond what you thought possible.

Am I cheerleading you? You bet I am! And I urge you to cheerlead others. We need to cheer for each other. Most people suffer from a deficit of good news, encouragement, and positive energy. It's hard to supply that for yourself, but not so hard to give it to someone else, while neuroscientists like Matthew Lieberman are proving what St. Francis said centuries ago: "In giving we receive."

We need each other. We need to get in the habit of giving routinely to each other, especially in a world that is silently separating us interpersonally, even as it joins us electronically. We need to preserve and promote human moments. We need to run the show, not let our devices run us.

There may have been a more exciting, uncertain time to be alive, but I can't think of one. The best way to take advantage of the teeming opportunities of our era is by learning how to master your mind, learning the skill of flexible focus, and tapping into the powers that positive energy and emotion can unleash, propelling you to do far more than you may have believed you could. And to hold, cherish, and develop what matters most.

epilogue

Ultimately, you will decide for yourself whether my solutions work better than what you're already doing. Speaking personally, I can tell you they've worked for me and my wife. We both have careers. My wife works part-time as a psychotherapist—she is a social worker by training—and does a great deal of volunteer work. I have an active private practice and also write books, this being my twentieth. We depend on our work to pay our bills, as neither of us has family money, and putting our three children through private schools and college (our youngest enrolled at Trinity in the fall of 2014) has taken most of what we otherwise would have saved. So we live from paycheck to paycheck.

While at times we feel overwhelmed, even desperate, we find ways to do what matters most to us and have some time to relax as well. This has cost us income to be sure—we have far less money than most of our friends—but has preserved our sanity and health, and kept us close as a family. My wife goes to the gym four days a week and has a regular dinner group, book group, exercise group, and just-because-we're-friends group. I go to the gym regularly as well, have a squash game I've been playing biweekly with the same man, my best friend, for over thirty years, and I watch a lot of TV, while my wife reads many books. We have always spent lots of time with our kids, be it family dinners, soccer games, school events, Sundays at the Patriots games (we've been season ticket holders since 1993), family vacations, or just hanging out. We live in a suburb of Boston, an area that is as high pressured and super-busy as any area in the country, with the possible exception of New York, where I also have an office and our daughter now lives.

All this is to say that I practice what I preach, and that I live in the midst of the world about which I write. I am not a dispassionate academic observing from the sidelines; I am very much in the game. And I have come to learn it is a game that need not overwhelm even its most intense players. Of course, more enlightened social policies would work wonders to allow more people to lead saner lives, such as universal child care or compensation for time spent as a caregiver or parent. That my wife and I have professional degrees makes earning a living far easier for us than for those who do not.

But I do believe that the solutions I outline in this book can help anyone who chooses to try them to reduce overload and regain sanity—and in so doing become more productive both at work and at home. Put simply, what's worked for me might work for you.

a word about ADHD and medications

In reading this book, especially chapter 6 about true ADHD, you might wonder if you yourself have ADHD. If you do have it, the chances are you don't know that you do because few doctors know how to diagnose ADHD in adults. Learning that you have ADHD is actually very good news, because the chances are excellent that treatment could dramatically change your life for the better.

Most adult ADHD is misdiagnosed as depression, an anxiety disorder, a personality disorder, an eating disorder, substance abuse, or a sex, gambling, or shopping addiction, or some or all of the above. At least 75 percent of ADHD in adults is never diagnosed. No condition in all of medicine has such a shocking lack of diagnosis. The science exists to diagnose adult ADHD, but the medical profession and the general public are insufficiently educated about it. This is a true tragedy, because there is no condition in all of the behavioral sciences where proper diagnosis and treatment can lead to a more dramatic improvement in a person's life. I have seen literally thousands of careers turn around, not to mention marriages saved, once the diagnosis of ADHD is made.

The major tip-off that you might be suffering from undiagnosed adult ADHD is *unexplained underachievement* coupled with *inconsistent performance*, flashes of brilliance, followed by lack of follow-through or a blank mind. If you see yourself or someone you know in this brief description, consult an expert who actually does understand ADHD. The consultation could dramatically change your life or the life of the person you know.

Since I specialize in treating ADHD, I've been prescribing medications to treat it for decades. I have enormous experience in their use, and I know exactly what good and what harm they can do. Given to the right patient in the right way, the medications can be a godsend. Given to the wrong patient or given in the wrong way, the medications can be dangerous, sometimes even lethal. The same is true, incidentally, of aspirin, penicillin, or water.

Two basic molecules are turned into the various stimulant medications currently available by prescription. All are controlled substances, highly regulated and supervised by a federal agency, the Drug Enforcement Administration (DEA).

One molecule is amphetamine (AMP). A Rhode Island doctor named Charles Bradley used it for the first time in the United States seventy-five years ago to treat what we now call ADHD. Bradley originally gave it to the behaviorally disturbed children on his unit to treat headaches, but, to his surprise, these children became far more focused and ambitious and less emotionally volatile after taking the pill. This was a great breakthrough not only in the treatment of ADHD, but in the understanding of the brain.

The other molecule is methylphenidate (MPH). First synthesized in 1944, it wasn't used to treat problems with focus until a scientist named

Leandro Panizzon, who worked for the pharmaceutical giant CIBA, developed a new version of it in 1954. He gave it to his wife to boost her blood pressure before she played tennis. Since her name was Rita, Panizzon named his concoction Ritaline. Today, it's simply called Ritalin. Rita found that the Ritaline not only boosted her blood pressure, but also improved her focus on the game.

These two molecules, put together in different ways to produce varying durations of action and methods of absorption and release, enter pharmacies as Ritalin, Ritalin LA (long-acting), Concerta (long-acting), Focalin, Focalin XR (long-acting), Metadate, and Daytrana (skin patch), all of which are forms of MPH; or Dexedrine, Dexedrine Spansules (long-acting), Adderall, Adderall XR (long-acting), or Vyvanse (long-acting), all forms of AMP. There is another prescription stimulant called Modafinil, marketed as Provigil, which is in a class of its own.

These drugs are not approved for the general public absent a diagnosis of ADHD. Since they are controlled substances, they can only be used in highly supervised, controlled settings. When used properly, each of these medications will increase mental focus in 80 percent of the patients who take them. Twenty percent of the time they won't work, or they cause intolerable side effects. All tend to suppress appetite. When I am prescribing, the only side effect I allow my patients to suffer is appetite suppression without unwanted weight loss. If the medication causes any other side effects—which may include elevated heart rate or blood pressure, agitation, headache, upset stomach, insomnia, tremor or tics, feelings of hyper-vigilance or paranoia, blunting of personality, or sedation—I ask the patient to discontinue the medication.

I only prescribe stimulants for people who have ADHD. If you are properly screened for ADHD and discover that you have it, don't feel bad about it. Adults with ADHD are typically highly creative, intuitive, entrepreneurial, pioneering, and innovative. They tend to think outside the box and be original and tenacious to the point of being stubborn.

They rarely give up. They also tend to have a marvelous sense of humor, a sparkle, and a certain charisma. What leads them to underachieve is inconsistent focus and a tendency to space out on details, time management, social niceties, and proper procedure.

What if someone who does not have ADHD takes a prescription stimulant? Usually they have improved focus, just as if someone who does not have a fever takes an aspirin and his body temperature decreases a small amount. But if someone who has a fever takes an aspirin, his body temperature decreases a great deal more. So, if someone who has ADHD takes a stimulant and it works, his ability to focus will improve much more than the person who does not have ADHD who takes a stimulant.

The media would have you believe that stimulants are overprescribed and dangerous. In fact, they are both under- and overprescribed. Many doctors won't prescribe stimulants because they "don't believe in ADHD," failing to comprehend that ADHD is not a religious principle but a well-researched scientific reality. Other doctors prescribe stimulants too frequently in the absence of a proper workup and diagnosis, leading to overprescribing. Stimulants used improperly can cause serious side effects, just as the misuse of any medication can. The media should better inform the general public so that people can appreciate the therapeutic power of stimulant medication and respect it as a useful intervention to be used with care.

Readers of this book may say, "I don't have ADHD, but I'd love to take a pill that would help me focus. Could a stimulant medication do that?" The answer is probably yes for most people, but stimulant medications are not currently approved by the FDA in the absence of the diagnosis of ADHD. The catch-22 here is that the vast majority of doctors know little or nothing about ADHD and how it appears in adults. So, as an adult, you can't get stimulant medication unless you have a diagnosis of ADHD, but you can't get a diagnosis of ADHD because most doctors, including specialists like psychiatrists and neurologists, don't know enough to recognize it.

over-the-counter medications, herbs, brain boosters

Now we enter into more confusing and controversial waters. Since so much money is at stake, as well as professional turf, it is difficult to nail down the truth about over-the-counter medications for ADHD.

The best source for explaining nonprescription brain boosters I've found is *Non-Drug Treatments for ADHD*, by Richard P. Brown, MD, and Patricia L. Gerbarg, MD, one a professor at Columbia University College of Physicians and Surgeons, and the other an assistant professor at New York Medical College.[1]

In my opinion, among the medications that improve focus that are available to the general public, caffeine is by far the best. Brown and Gerbarg disagree with me, citing the many side effects caffeine can have. They recommend instead various herbs, roots, and other natural substances, and cite solid research to back up their claims. Among the substances they tout most highly are: Rhodiola rosea, Ayurvedic herbs, Bacopa monnieri, Ginkgo biloba, Ginseng, Pycnogenol, and combinations of these marketed under various trade names. You can be your own experimental animal. Just check with your doctor first, and try not to spend a lot of money on what is unproven. And I would suggest you read Brown and Gerbarg's book.

Some patients tell me that a quick sniff of peppermint oil helps them focus, or heating rosemary oil so the scent diffuses through the workplace helps keep people alert.

It makes sense to first use what's proven, but to keep an open mind for other possibilities. Just be careful, because the world of natural, alternative, whole, or whatever other buzzword adjective gets applied is a shifty entrepreneur's dream come true: millions of eager, gullible customers in a field with little regulation.

Nonetheless, only by keeping an open mind have I learned the value of many of the suggestions in this book, and created my practice as a focus doctor, a specialty that didn't exist until modern life created the need for it.

NOTES

INTRODUCTION

1. Ann Crittenden, "On Top of Everything Else: A journalist, wife, and mother searches for answers to our headlong descent into multitasking madness," *New York Times Book Review*, March 30, 2014.

2. Tim Armstrong, conversation with author, May 2, 2014.

3. The official diagnostic manual covers only ADHD. It has two subtypes: primarily inattentive or combined. The primarily inattentive subtype is ADHD without the *H*, without the symptom of hyperactivity. It is what the general public calls ADD. The combined subtype includes the symptom of hyperactivity, so it is ADHD with the *H*. Unnecessarily confusing? Yes, indeed.

4. Leslie Taylor, "Price Tag for Lost Productivity: $544 Billion," *Inc.*, August 21, 2006, http://www.inc.com/news/articles/200608/time.html.

5. See http://iorgforum.org/research/.

6. American Psychological Association, "Multitasking: Switching costs," March 20, 2006, http://www.apa.org/research/action/multitask.aspx.

7. Herb Ruckle, MD, Loma Linda University, e-mail to author, February 8, 2014.

8. José Ortega y Gasset, *The Revolt of the Masses* (New York: W.W. Norton, 1993), 21.

9. Daniel Goleman, *Focus: The Hidden Driver of Excellence* (New York: HarperCollins, 2013).

10. Nikos Kazantzakis, *Zorba the Greek* (New York: Simon & Schuster, 1953).

CHAPTER 1

1. Linda Stone on her website lindastone.net.

2. American Psychiatric Association, *Diagnostic and Statistical Manual of Mental Disorders, 5th Edition: DSM-5* (Arlington, VA: American Psychiatric Association, 2013), 795–796.

3. National Institute on Drug Abuse, www.drugabuse.gov.

4. Lance Dodes, MD, and Zachary Dodes, *The Sober Truth: Debunking the Bad Science behind the 12-Step Programs and the Rehab Industry* (Boston: Beacon Press, 2014), 92.

5. E. J. Khantzian and M. J. Albanese, *Understanding Addiction as Self-Medication: Finding Hope Behind the Pain* (London; New York: Rowman & Littlefield, 2008).

CHAPTER 3

1. Søren Kierkegaard, *The Sickness Unto Death*, 1849.

2. Kathy Kolbe, *Conative Connection: Acting on Instincts* (New York: Addison-Wesley, 1989).

3. Carol Dweck, *Mindset: The New Psychology of Success* (New York: Random House, 2007).

CHAPTER 4

1. Building on the work of Ernest Becker, whose book *The Denial of Death* won the Pulitzer Prize in 1973, Sheldon Solomon, Tom Pyszczynski, and Jeff Greenberg have performed experiments showing how terror at the prospect of one's mortality deeply influences much of human behavior and beliefs.

2. See Bessel Van der Kolk, *Traumatic Stress: The Effects of Overwhelming Experience on Mind, Body, and Society* (New York: Guilford Press, 1996).

3. Susan Nolen-Hoeksema et al., "Rethinking Rumination," *Perspectives on Psychological Science* 3, no. 5 (2008): 400–424.

4. C. Fabbri et al., "Genetics of serotonin receptors and depression: state of the art," *Current Drug Targets* 14, no. 5 (2013): 531–548.

5. Norbert Bonhomme and Ennio Esposito, "Involvement of Serotonin and Dopamine in the Mechanism of Action of Novel Anti-Depressant Drugs: A Review," *Journal of Clinical Psychopharmacology* 18, no. 6 (1998): 447–454.

6. Nicholas Christakis and James Fowler report on their survey of 3,000 randomly selected Americans. They found that "the average American has just four close social contacts, with most having between two and six. Sadly, 12 percent of Americans listed no one with whom they could discuss important matters or spend free time. At the other extreme, 5 percent of Americans had eight such people." See Nicholas A. Christakis and James H. Fowler, *Connected: The Surprising Power of Social Networks and How They Shape Our Lives* (New York: Little, Brown, 2009), 18.

CHAPTER 5

1. Christopher Lasch, *The Culture of Narcissism: American Life in an Age of Diminishing Expectations* (New York: W.W. Norton, 1991); and Jean M. Twenge and W. Keith Campbell, *The Narcissism Epidemic: Living in the Age of Entitlement* (New York: Simon & Schuster, 2013).

2. Marie Brenner, conversation with author, New York City, July 10, 2013.

3. See James Adrioni, "Impure Altruism and Donations to Public Goods," *Royal Economic Society Economic Journal* (1990), http://www.jstor.org/discover/10.2307/2234133?uid=3739952&uid=2&uid=4&uid=3739256&sid=21102183246833.

4. Edward O. Wilson, *The Social Conquest of Earth* (New York: W.W. Norton, 2012), 117.

5. Rachel Bachner-Melman et al., "Dopaminergic Polymorphisms Associated with Self-Report Measures of Human Altruism: A Fresh Pheonotype for the Dopamine D4 Receptor," *Molecular Psychiatry* 10, no. 4 (2005): 333–335.

6. J. Moll et al., "Human fronto-mesolimbic networks guide decisions about charitable donation," *Proceedings of the National Academy of Sciences* 103, no. 42 (2006): 15623–15628; cited by Mathew Lieberman, *Social: Why Our Brains Are Wired to Connect* (New York: Crown, 2006), 90.

7. St. Francis of Assisi, *The Writings of St. Francis of Assisi*, trans. Father Paschel Robinson (Philadelphia: Dolphin Press, 1906).

8. Peter Frost and Sandra Robinson, "Toxic Handler: Organizational Hero—and Casualty," HBR *OnPoint* Enhanced Edition, January 2002, http://hbr.org/product/toxic-handler-organizational-hero-and-casualty-hbr-onpoint-enhanced-edition/an/8571-PDF-ENG.

9. Anna Freud, *The Ego and the Mechanisms of Defense* (London: Karnac Books, 2011), Kindle edition.

10. Ibid., location 1327 of 2171 in Kindle edition.

11. William James, from a letter to W. Lutoslawski, in *The Letters of William James, edited by his son, Henry James*, vol. II (Boston: Atlantic Monthly Press, 1920), 252.

12. José Ortega y Gasset, *Revolt of the Masses*, 156–157.

CHAPTER 7

1. Matthew Lieberman, *Social: Why Our Brains Are Wired to Connect* (New York: Crown, 2013), 25.

2. Mihaly Csikszentmihalyi, *Beyond Boredom and Anxiety: Experiencing Flow in Work and Play* (San Francisco: Jossey-Bass, 1975).

3. W. B. Yeats, "Among School Children," 1928.

4. Steven Kotler, *The Rise of Superman: Decoding the Science of Ultimate Human Performance* (Seattle: Amazon Publishing, 2014).

5. Steven Kotler, conversations with author, 2013.

6. Jeffrey H. Dyer, Hal B. Gregersen, and Clayton M. Christensen, *The Innovator's DNA: Mastering the Five Skills of Disruptive Innovators* (Boston: Harvard Business Review Press, 2011).

7. Robert Frost, "The Road Not Taken," 1916.

8. Adrian Bejan and J. Peder Zane, *Design in Nature: How the Constructal Law Governs Evolution in Biology, Physics, Technology, and Social Organization* (New York: Doubleday, 2012).

9. Ibid., 2.

10. Ibid., 3.

11. Louis Pasteur, quoted in René Vallery-Radot, *The Life of Pasteur* (New York: Doubleday, Page & Company, 1927).

12. Jim Loehr and Tony Schwartz, *The Power of Full Engagement* (New York: Free Press, 2003).

CHAPTER 8

1. James D. Laird, *Feelings: The Perception of Self* (Oxford and New York: Oxford University Press, 2007).

2. DrowsyDriving.org Facts and Stats, accessed July 17, 2014, http://drowsydriving.org/about/facts-and-stats/.

3. Vatsal Thakkar, "Diagnosing the Wrong Deficit," *New York Times*, April 28, 2013.

4. David K. Randall, *Dreamland: Adventures in the Strange Science of Sleep* (New York: W.W. Norton, 2012), 27–29.

5. Jeffrey H. Larson, D. Russell Crane, and Craig W. Smith, "Morning and Night Couples: The Effect of Wake and Sleep Pattern on Marital Adjustment," *Journal of Marital & Family Therapy* 17, no. 1 (January 1991): 53–65.

6. See Brett McKay and Kate McKay, "Unleash the Power of the Nap," *The Art of Manliness* (website), http://www.artofmanliness.com/2011/02/07/unleash-the-power-of-the-nap/; and Nikki Waller, "On Our Radar: The Office Nap Room," *The Wall Street Journal* online, http://blogs.wsj.com/atwork/2013/03/12/on-our-radar-the-office-nap-room/.

7. T. Colin Campbell et al., *The China Study: The Most Comprehensive Study of Nutrition Ever Conducted and the Startling Implications for Diet* (Dallas, TX: BenBella Books, 2004).

8. For more on going gluten-free, see http://www.mayoclinic.com/health/gluten-free-diet/my01140.

9. "Supplements: A scorecard," *Harvard Men's Health Watch,* April 2012, http://www.health.harvard.edu/newsletters/harvard_mens_health_watch/2012/April/supplements-a-scorecard.

10. Michel Lucas et al., "Coffee, Caffeine, And Depression Among Women," *JAMA Internal Medicine*, 171, no. 17: (September 26, 2011), http://archinte.jamanetwork.com/article.aspx?articleid=1105943.

11. See "How Exercise Can Lead to a Better Brain," *New York Times*, April 18, 2012, http://www.nytimes.com/2012/04/22/magazine/how-exercise-could-lead-to-a-better-brain.html?pagewanted=all&_r=0.

12. John Ratey, *Spark: The Revolutionary New Science of Exercise and the Brain* (New York: Little, Brown, 2008).

CHAPTER 9

1. Michael Carroll, *The Mindful Leader: Awakening Your Natural Management Skills Through Mindfulness Meditation* (Boston: Trumpeter Books, 2007).

2. Patricia Marx, American Chronicles, "Mentally Fit: Workouts at the Brain Gym," *The New Yorker*, July 29, 2013, 24.

3. B.P. = Brad Pitt; N.L. = Norman Lear; R.W. = Robert Wright; and T.A. = Tim Allen.

CHAPTER 10

1. Matthew Lieberman, *Social: Why Our Brains Are Wired to Connect* (New York: Crown, 2013), 267.

2. Stephanie Pappas, "Early Neglect Alters Kids' Brains," *Livescience.com,* July 23, 2012, http://livescience.com/21778-early-neglect-alters-kids-brains.html.

3. L. F. Berkman, "The Role of Social Relations in Health Promotion," *Psychosomatic Medicine* 57, no. 3 (1995): 245–254.

4. Led by professors James Anderson and, after him, Stuart Schreiber, the Harvard chemistry department revamped its culture from one characterized by isolation and disconnection to a far more connected culture following the suicide of a gifted graduate student in 1998. I was involved in this effort as a consultant for five years. Anderson and Schreiber deserve immense credit for taking the problem of disconnection as seriously as they did.

5. Nicholas A. Christakis and James H. Fowler, *Connected*, 18.

6. Ibid., 22.

7. Ibid., 31.

8. Ibid., 35.

9. Ibid., 49.

10. George Vaillant, *Adaptation to Life* (Boston: Little, Brown, 1977).

11. Attributed to Rabbi Hyman Schachtel.

CHAPTER 11

1. "Type 'D' for distressed," *Harvard Heart Letter*, August 2005, http://www.health .harvard.edu/newsweek/Type_D_for_distressed.htm.

2. Aaron Sorkin, *A Few Good Men*, directed by Rob Reiner (Castle Rock, 1992).

3. Epictetus, *The Enchiridion*, compiled by Flavius Arrianus, ca. 90 AD, trans. Nicholas P. White (Indianapolis/Cambridge: Hackett Publishing Company, 1983), 13.

4. Ibid.

CHAPTER 12

1. James Boswell, *Life of Johnson*, ed. George Birbeck Hill (Public Domain Book, 1791, 1887).

2. Dan Sullivan, conversation with author, New York City, August 14, 2013.

3. Steven Kotler, *The Rise of Superman: Decoding the Science of Ultimate Human Performance* (Seattle: Amazon Publishing, 2014), 290.

4. This example and those that follow can all be found at www.thefuntheory.com.

CHAPTER 13

1. Joseph Wood Krutch, *The Modern Temper* (New York: Harcourt Brace & Company, 1929), 114.

APPENDIX

1. Richard P. Brown, MD, and Patricia L. Gerbarg, MD, *Non-Drug Treatments for ADHD* (New York: W.W. Norton, 2012).

INDEX

ACKNOWLEDGMENTS

Many people contributed to *Driven to Distraction at Work*, far more than I can possibly thank individually here. This book was longer in the making than any of my previous volumes because I needed to consult with so many people in diverse fields. Let me extend a heartfelt thank you to all of you who took the time to discuss with me the many elements of focus, attention, and the modern workplace.

Let me also thank the many patients of mine who contributed to the stories in the book. I learned so much from all of you; I can hardly tell you how much. Although your identities are all disguised, I hope you see the fruits of our labors represented well on these pages.

When I hit a roadblock in writing, my friend and editor par excellence, Bronwyn Fryer, stepped in and got the book back on track. Without her help I could not have completed this project.

Let me also thank the exceptional team at Harvard Business Review Press, led by my ever-encouraging editor, Melinda Merino, and her superb supporting cast, including Erin Brown, Courtney Cashman, Dave Lievens, Nina Nocciolino, and copyeditor Jane Gebhart.

And, of course, my everlasting thanks go to my agent of twenty years, Jill Kneerim, and her phenomenal group at Kneerim, Williams & Bloom in Boston, especially Hope Denekamp, an ideal in so many ways.

Finally, as always, my deepest debt and greatest thanks go to my wife of twenty-five years, Sue, and our three kids, Lucy, now twenty-five; Jack, twenty-two; and Tucker, nineteen. They make my life shine. I should also thank another member of our troupe, our incomparable Jack Russell, Ziggy, who never ceases to make us all love life just a bit more.

ABOUT THE AUTHOR

EDWARD M. HALLOWELL, MD, runs the Hallowell Centers in Sudbury, Massachusetts, New York City, and San Francisco, all specializing in training attention in people of all ages. He lives in the Boston area with his wife, Sue. Their three children have all left the nest as of 2014, so they are adapting to a different life! Visit his website at drhallowell.com.